TESTAMENTUM:

TWO ALPHABETS

Iván Argüelles

Cyberwit.net
HIG 45 Kaushambi Kunj, Kalindipuram
Allahabad - 211011 (U.P.) India
http://www.cyberwit.net
Tel: +(91) 9415091004 +(91) (532) 2552257
E-mail: info@cyberwit.net

Printed at Repro India Limited.

(α)

Zeu pater ! at what stage of love-making
did you regain consciousness ? forged realities
littered nesses and rocky inlets mountains
and wild inaccessible to the light fastnesses
what is to wake for ? deceit and fraud
copulate with myth to distort memory
of learning to write and to go to bed and
say nightly prayers and look to the window
for an escape route to legendary auras
exhausted I lay my inks down and set
the old stone in place behind the garden
where a worn path leads in circles to the
source of life small gooseberry bushes
emerging from the snow and a smudge
of grey against the finger-thin horizon
it is to say goodbye here shivering and lost
listening for a traffic of pyramids amid
enigmas and puzzles formation of language
fragments of a statue never to be completed
ruin of thought misshapen vowels aphasia
of the senses a lingering in the half-lamp
of reason turning away from the Design
to lesser islands with tutelary deities
temples eaten by the lye of time unfamiliar
steps leading only partially to the heavens
pinnacle of being ! has come and gone
this once of breathing easily leaning on
the salt and bastion of the imagination
to find the street and its egress through maps

and hospitals and unkempt terraces and greens
what is the reading program for my last 10 years
and to whom can I tender questions ?
the Catalan mysteries the song of Santa Eulalia
half-frozen in time the denizens of the alley
where the Atlas of the Universe was discovered
and shadows and unprinted matter and what
can never be answered always *there*
la stagione morta
to count one's dead almagest and portfolio
interleaved between thumb and thumb
the whole sum of the skies captured instamatically
before the eye can blink the downfall of angels
dust-storms in upheaval rival cities *Boom !*
gray and wave reaping mists weaving reef
and horizon foredriven rains anguish and axolotl
walking past the dark portal of the *Catholic* temple
on the shortest day of the year counting one's
dead the season unsung one hand missing
the other intricately stuttering into a rosary
five times fifty and then some the cadavers
of rose and narcissus and hyacinth heaped up
for the pyre a confinement of cloud and asterism
smoke in alphabets rising warning flags vacancies
memorial services chants for the dead *resurrection*
standing as I am beyond the perimeter
faint whiff of gasoline the cold whetstone
its companions umbrella and empty whiskey bottle
skeleton of a garage fishing poles ice in flakes
dirty like fish scales on the worn pavement
leading out slowly toward sunset golden
flush against the winter bleak hills to the west
la stagione morta
for no one

(β)

landscape of river sedge and palms
clearly and blue of cyanide paste on the walls
brightly bedecked the 15th century BC
to the south temple of Phaistos and its hills
wild fowl and tall reeds the still summer of a day
out of time the forgeries of thought and innocence
shimmering the mosaic of sky as a gift to Thutmose
the plain chant in the ear as prepares the hour
of recognition and to proceed with the investigation
grass and meadow insects underneath a goddess
whose enormous shadow the shape of an axe
spreads across the broad way on either side
the mind gathers in its knots of fruit and petals
damp against the brow and may I ask just who ?
issuing from the carved niche where a statuette
they pray nightly to it the princesses and
by day in big hair and fobs and bellows going
full steam and wearing furlongs of silken stuff
edges of sapphire small pearled fingers
making straight for the oblong structure sunken
just slightly will listen to the reading of reefs
wreathes mansions of air tinted sepia
have gathered from the nearby sea cuttlefish
and small pink shells laced into fans or
even in oil float small likenesses of ships bearing
captives who are shaking dust from their tasks
leaning their spears against the moonlight
until today so little of the known world revealed
put on this mask try on this footwear tie these

greaves around *thy* shins ! have been dreaming
asleep in the same page for close to eight decades
still time to read the *Punica* of Silius Italicus
batteries and fuses that connect light
to the architectures of rain the soft falling
though crystal rose-colored haze hand held
the folding fan with orients of Phrygian embroideries
simulacra of Helen in white nephrite stone
when they have finished sculpting the afternoon
wave over heat and polished around the edges
a map of the water that girdles the earth
and wearing serpents on the upper arms dance
projecting into the waning sunlight promises
of ink of subterranean mysteries of vapors
trying to wake from this heavy hour can hear
the islands ringing and the new drum skins
tattooing the wind with graven images
talk of gramophones and motor-wheels
depictions of the mountain to the east of the indies
where they say priests can read in nectar
the signs of the dead long curlicues and dots
spotting the exterior of a massive hide left to tan
withering and fragments with a form of writing
a population of up to one hundred thousand glyphs
hot ginger on the tongue and memory of
Sri Lanka where monkeys do Vedic mantras
in reverse tusk and emblem of a higher planet
so many are the detours bypaths hill slopes
deviations of the texts intersections of red vowels
loud and looping deep into the brain's ear
the entire southern direction of space immersed
in the fragrant tank overrun with ivy and musk
have fallen half dead again in the foyer

a library of corrupted syllables echoing
vague and boundless as the month before time
they take the palms of their hands
and set them against the fever
hauling from the quarry thighs of marble
ancient systems of depth
I am among *them*

(γ)

flight of twelve steps forty-five feet broad
roof over roof imposing though smaller
on the arid hillside paintings of such exquisite
refinement where have these delicacies fled
like Hecuba barking like a rabid dog
all her sons turned to ashes and the signals
from on high prayers to the rulers of the cosmos
colored their faces or covered them with soot
not even the Chinese could disentangle
from a mesh of etymologies a poetry as
concise as it was enigmatic pieced together by
syllables sewn to retroflex consonants
meant to be pronounced on nights of full moon
Phoebe hold thy *Splendor !* walk the distance
feel the cold slowly possessing the body
marmoreal slabs laid out in a geometrical figure
if one could interpret these archaic efforts
at dialoguing with the divinities sprawling
their rock fragments out in a cryptic formation
discernible only from a considerable height
then and only then did I feel a faint nausea
about to fall from the precipice and remembering
something that could never have happened to me
drawing a long train of precious cloth
over the flagstones mysterious and feminine
in appearance vatic utterances and a shining
at the end of a long corridor small torches
flickering like eyelids on the term of death
could realize the library's extent then rising
above the other structures and for up to eight decades

sat there writing and rewriting the selfsame ode
the upper windows without panes like balconies
imagine the brow depicted with stags running
and the fleet shafts aimed for the dummy bird
tied to the highest branch of the spreading plane tree
palms and the sound of a water rushing unseen
can you remember that afternoon as well ?
someone came out of the narrow alleyway
bearing a tray with towels and tufts and grape bunches
the color of the northern sea you could hear
wave over wave pressing the infinite echo
in houses that resemble contemporary Egyptian ones
faces seen elusive as graphs or symbols and some
sat around in a circling hunkering blowing
into conch shells for the future to be more vivid
earthen pots burnt and hardened with sketches
of some holding shields and spears others
diving head first into the maw of Hades
each with an inner courtyard walled on three sides
to find the right address and enter with
offerings sometimes only paper or rattles
for the *Magna Dea* long hours of circular heat
and darkness unable to understand
or to restrain the imagination from going
crazy hearing those gongs and sistra non-stop
until evening the cool shadows penetrated
even into the labyrinth where the captive mind
ululating the repetitive syllables meant
to release the poor burdened soul
into the infinite night air
shivers and whispers
gone

(δ)

nights ovoid in shape and indefinite the swamp
slushing sound a rhetoric of windows outside
the ear to reassemble the impositions of vowel
within the dried brick foundation building
upwards of forty stories a structure elusive and
peaked with a white surf and visible for years
until exhausted the aim got lost in the plethora
of detail the historian with his lathe and tumult
describing each dynasty with long ciceronian periods
a dismay to reader and librarian alike footnotes
deltas asteroids commas delusional full-stops
the very attempt to dream within such small parameters
switches and envy of the gods in their cradle of ire
HIPPOPOTAMUS AND LOTUS submerged in pools
strangled by algae green and blue writhing symptoms
Amon Ra his left hoof first a peal of thunder a flea
the fashionable idiom with shorter hemline the stars
patched here and there the loose paragraph afloat
miles from the *Ear-of-Dionysos* in Siracusa in the rain
sedge and palm and egrets aloof on one leg daring
the woof of clouds a tempest of consonants falling
out of their hieroglyphic order and a page turning
in the silence of a finger where the light bleeds from
the little oil wicks flickering in the aorist tense a
lunation of hours of days and months the Great Year
with its constellations of IBIS AND CROCODILE
the humid archipelago or the delicate isthmus
ready to snap in half given the right chisel blow
ants swarming beneath the deity's left eyelid

electricity of horses swart and sleek in the Dawn
of creation south of the Metropolis of the Dead
luminous zip-code acres of pampas grass lying down
praying to the harrowing winds of Nemesis who
is either fastening or unfastening her shoulder *fibbia*
bared skin glistening and the accompanying grief
was human ever meant to surpass itself in Harmony ?
yet do the gloomy throngs go unwinding down the
steep to the Stygian bank a lament as unintelligible
as it is heart-rending do these days of endless moan
and long afternoons within the ruins each stone a
letter to be deciphered and then to sleep in dust
anchored the mind to the flitting dream of being
on thy careless brow such words shall I engrave
ISIS MUMTAZ MAHAL BEATRICE

(ε)

in the end we only know things *partially*
do we memorize the sounds but not the meaning ?
palace fortified on the rocky summit gazing to
the grayish groves all around beneath and a
subterranean pathway leading up to the high gate
men's quarters slightly larger than the women's
a courtyard and altar set for offerings where
sunlight splashes fierce by midday
if but memory were more complete the full day
of time the restless hours needled by the hand
of some swart and unknown deity that has revealed
a way of keeping track the number of urns filled
and the greater of men felled at first pressed
into hot wax and later on hardening clay
do you recall that time on the shoreline watching
from above the graceful swooping of gulls
silvery wings flashing on the margins of light
who was calling out whose profound face appeared
from the moorings and tackle unshaven by
a few days and as swiftly disappeared a voice
no ear had before kenned a great sorrow came
upon us that was the knowledge of death
whenever I drive by steering my vehicle
and look up I espy the windows the last home
of his body and cry out to some nefarious and
chthonic deity the why and the wherefore
of the mortal limb and only the rains and the smoke
inter the image and the wheel that bore it
the drawing grafted on to the skin of air

shows a palace replete with intricate chambers
a place for drinking and one for jousting
and numerous the bed rooms the wine cellars
the entrance in fact to the other world hard by
the fresh springlet at the back gate where
a supply of water is always available where
they wash their hands and feet before entering
and there is a sacred hush and a darkening
even at noon and the ushering of the spirit
through walls and doorways both and a spot
recently painted depicting the descent of the souls
intently as we stare into the Design it makes
little sense we wonder and wander hearing
echoes from the archaic times from rock
and grass and the springing forth from earth
fully armored the cast of soldiers in the glint
of an early afternoon and as we age sit ourselves
on hard benches applying the mind to letters
difficult to apprehend sometimes nothing more
than squiggles fading red dots slashes and marks
thumb-prints on brittle parchment or palm-leaf
these ought to be the names of gods some
originating in the fertile deltas others out of
mountains carved with wings that transport
them from mind to mind into the Orient
but in the end it is despair and little else
that sustains us breathing in the dusty arcana
lost in some reach of the ruins settled high
on the rocky summit a struggle to remember
what it was and why we mourned so
our bodies like sacks cast against the stone
our thoughts as ever incomplete a knowledge
less than partial and the enormous avenues of sleep
night with its flickering code of stars

(ζ)

emerged incomplete as human figures out of stone
in spirit speaking as if alive with the full content
of mind the enormous poetry of thoughts unassembled
words and meters and strange melodies pointing
into the air and clouds slowly tumbling
out of the oracle imprecise the sound of motors
growling underground it seemed wasted and wan
our bodies as well and prescriptions and graphs
and the wavering lines going up and down
indicating the warning and monitor of breath
did Zeus just once manifest as an eagle swooping ?
are there things more magnificent than the sea of being ?
the magma the miasma the treacherous misstep
to the left the vista now hazy of the olive groves
terraced and divided into great slabs the rock
formations littered with scrawls of mortal passage
sphinxes griffins and consciousness itself depicted
and women waving their hands from a finely wrought
balcony and sandstone and ivory and tombs cut
into the hill of a porous substance and smoke in ladders
colored marble and sections to resemble delicate
floral patterns on a great southern stream so
flowing and we watched it all passing in a dream
review shadowy and zigzagging up the mountain
representations of the long gone in ancestral robes
lichen and moss in the eye orbits and a reading
aloud of the noon registers hieroglyph and postern
gates flung wide open on rusty pins if only we could
you and I the twin of the map scrawl a driven

and the antiquities of rain and moon drizzle each
a hand closer to the form of paradise and doves
accompanying the female form the enormous shape
of ink held still for the camera eye and the plates
copper strewn between the leaves and soon it would
be the thought-styles of the neolithic and borrowings
from Sumer not of the vowels but of the firmament
drawn in primitive clusters the consonants a-glitter
like stars or phonetic orders climbing in sound
what could it ever mean even as we keep dying
holding on to the cloths and tints trying to intercept
memory at its midpoint a cave of echoes and thumbs
digests and recordings of lunations a variegated
yes you are still struggling with the recall of grass
sighted on knolls or lampshades at twilight glowing
in the distance of a home long held vacant a darkness
knit between the incomplete lexica of the mind
spotted panther and bull on either side with regalia
and fancy tapestries laid over the burnished floors
the words for *brother* and *dandelion* engraved on
the far side of the cup and deep rich the drafts
of wine imported from far Lycia do we know at all
where we are today what it stands for the voices
coming out of the neighbor's radio and if we turn
and the pages have no text a funeral chamber to
the right and woven damask hangings and silver
worked into the threads the faint harmonies
having no direction taking us to inner quarters
lacking windows only a rush-light cut into the ceiling
sleep we will here side by side each of us no more
than dust mounds heaped against the base
listening for the careers of summer insects drilling
into the somnolent ear-maze a flute a thin reedy note

and the missing partners lost in the violence
and powders of war a long unwinding sea-wave

(η)

carbon cycles and turgid amniotic seas distances
level with the street of the Greek restaurants
and the hospital across the way born of a winter
with archaic structures of snow and mourning to *be*
here lies the sibyl Erophile *next to nymphs and Hermes*
who never lost her sovereignty among tribes called
birds or robbers untouchables and sinners
fan-shaped leaves bordered by rosettes and
underground clefts bearing water from the marsh
as far as Nubia // the language of the *Furies*
impenetrable syllables somewhere between Dog-Latin
Burial-Etruscan and the Italian of the Vita Nuova
as if listening to stone while asleep and wafting
gold leaf over sky weave and the portents and warnings
no girl under twelve can a Sybil be nor lay to rust
her shadow and all along the shades of Tantalus
and Thyestes and the myriad speeches of statues
brought to life by the deft hand of Daedalus
far to the left of the page's margin dusts of the Orient
sealed with the names of the god-head *Œ̃a* and *Uma*
and a fortress build in the Cretan style hiring painters
from the Delta or Cyprus but no activity be it reading
the Classics or idling in a stream drugged on *Bang*
can stave off the ultimate and hymn we then to heavens
appeals and plaints and demands for justice of the
states and governments that are hell-bent on Ruin
universal and final and the atmospheres rising heavy
today and turgid with the botany of unreason and ire
and the manifold phantoms the recent dead the *child*
in his house of cellophane and wadding and the furious

intent to close off the oceans with their generations
of discolored algae and coral and the *Quean* who will
shift in her paramount anger from a cinema of beauty
to one of Chaos and Nemesis the double simulacra
wielding swords of twin-edged Light and fanning
on the peaks of Caria and Lydia their small philosophies
of routine and ennui // playwright of the damned
Seneca in his hot bath easing his mind of breath
other words from his century include *Caelum* and *Styx*
we pitiful remnants bordering our sidewalks with human
offal and a syntax of solar homophones too bright
for mortal consciousness the worm and the mite
in the center of the diagram when all else fails
and a telephone call to the Emergency Number
and we await the recitation of the Siren and the vision
of the *Pearl* and so many once the tender and visceral
memories of infancies in gold embroideries and
sunsets more Spanish than the color of citrus
a minute on this side of the inch and the nights
descend with a canvas of painted palms and sedge
the soothing hemline there lay the head and sleep
listening to the wandering streams issuing
from the myth of rock and dew-drop
and from them the soul arising

(θ)

we can make up words ascribe false etymologies
to air and physics and to the memorials in stone
erected by the Cyclops and go back to childhoods
when summer was in fission and the clouds of steam
and the orient of the ineffable Sun before creation
we can so many other phrases aspire reading deep
into the quarrels between god and god over the soul
and fix the tiny niches each with a troubling goddess
a map of hair so immense the cosmos does not fit
contours and allure the mind rejects its brain to die
how gorgeous the first Dawn the horses like paragraphs
born of a single flame riding over the unborn thought
and seize the moment with shadowy hands of sound
linking echo to memory of itself rebounding from
rock to ness and craggy distant defiles worlds unknown
but to those who sleep in the buried arm of Aphrodite
and pine away for newer words for syllables none
can pronounce and fashion forms of writing using
sand and pumice and waters that engender rust and sing
loud the shapeless metal that hovers in the lesser sky
myths that breed grief and mourning too and the abscess
that opens the cranium to a flowering of fevered light
how came we to this Hour to this fractured instant
to this parallel of language and silence bereft of tone
is what the thermometer sees a word ? is beyond the
girded edge of rock another earth nameless and deaf ?
burnished floors garlands crowning statuary heads
long columns and corridors straight the Path to hell
guide us then some pale Phoebe armless in her fading

splendor her circuits of baffling fog and nerve gone
and bind the brow with dark ivy tightening dismay
the goat-foot that strikes tragedy its first note and
from some errant stone expect the oracle to emerge
difficult to grasp haunting vowels emissions woven
in the turbulent morning colors and from afar
come messages in recent languages and conjectures
that this will be the last to hover in the sky a signal
flashing on and off in a recollection of clinic and void
you too will come to this and build a mound and firmly
into the clayey soil strike a single consonant a magic
wrapped in a circumflex of doubt and gather tribes
of ghosts hungry and bloodless and shale and shingle
overhead and listen for the southern winds to howl
bringing down mighty painted walls of enduring
to the ground and shadow over shadow in the glade
and whispers of ankles running swiftly over grass
how can there be *names* for this ? inventions of mind
tempests of synapse and severed sinew and cries
engulfing the territories once ruled by Sarpedon
remote provinces of Sleep and Death now ant-heaps
dormant spires of mirage and delirium the *Alas !*
of misfortune and wagering on the stock market
had we but words to renew what knowledge we have lost
and meter and rhythm to drum a dance of time
wild soliloquy of Pluto raving in his dream of white
his child-bride at his knee his Parent in divided Ire
alive alone either one of us quizzing the lexica of space
no answer no response from the tacit robe that drapes
entrance to the Platonic cave

(ι)

a few small bee-hive tombs and beside them
the larger mound the tumulus of Valum Votan
false-necked jars and scarab of Queen *Taia*
shards scratched initials broken flint spear heads
et cetera was here the charred remains of the
tenth version of the city and how many versions
can there be if there is only One Mystery
hod-carriers and water buckets shoulders
primed for emotional delivery on this side
plainly great walls erected over lesser ones still
burning after all these centuries weaving in
and out of bodies the breath and animus
writing one's memoirs on a thumb nail
these are the months when the dead return
these are the very days without reflection
winters steeped in thumbs of ice and carts
struggling with their oxen and fleas and lice
consuming what they can of what the eye sees
and twice or thrice called out in brittle air
and saw the vowels freeze into contours
names of divinities and votaries sacrificed
in tales and remembrances encapsulated in
solidified steam high in the dawn's raking light
how to come back how to reorganize birth
how to justify the misplaced consonant growing
hard in its dense soil of disappearances and
moving slowly over the earth of many dynasties
trowel in hand looking to scrape the very spot
they say he spent the ghost delivering its heights

to the Messenger with the winged sandals to
be transported to the enormous southland
where variations of sand and ink and tumult
the clouds of origination warring with flame
stand emblazoned in a universal memory
masonry of air and scaffolding of ether
monuments of a ruder time emblems a
single hand might hold yielding the phantom
to the furies of its conscience and the difficulties
of navigation and to speak no more of this
for a man's life is nothing but a cigarette
puffed just once & extinguished in a glass ashtray
in the confines of a gaudy and cheap hotel room
no less a mortal was Valum Votan in his jazz
round about the elysian nymphs the altars and
incense hillsides and youth a romp in coppices
and groves where afternoons extend a wan sunlight
into the nooks and recesses and voices might be
heard and the graphs of a numinous choir
taking from the shaking leaves their febrile life
and giving it back to the sundered darkness
these are the months when the dead return
the dead who have never left us

(κ)

Apollo—god of Mice! hear us out
doctors and doctors for the rash of human
failings and buddhas and more buddhas
wearing bright Nepali spirit masks
driving home the root and swirling sounds
high above the creaking Wain rumbling
through the Pleiades and the haunting rains
the restless memories downpours and cold
wintery blasts glasses shatter and bodies
in the tumult of existence how they ache
and moaning through the night to caress
again just once the soft before tumbling
downwards into the fated hells of yore
will you come with me and search the books
for a page that will not turn and read
the passage of the fairy lore the myths
of days when kings ruled with malt and
pride bearing scepters like bending reeds
and played the hour through a game
of dice or with their retinue retired
for the sacred hunt fearing to strike
by mistake the Goddess awful in her bath
wet and brilliant in the raving light
Oh there are other worlds to deny and
weathers that destroy by birth all hope
seasons that come and go in a single leaf
and voices torn from the tongue at night
predicting the lessons of the distant sea
loss without recovery lives gone before

their color fills and heavens of mendacity
gods expurgated for their treachery and
whim and isolated in sealed urns and vats
oils and grains messages of the other earth
children sprung from a grassy knoll loud
with glee and frolic their fragile shadows
already know the end before the needle's spent
the famous rides back and forth on vehicles
driven by the furious merchants of melody
resounding vowels and echoes fit for no ear
the assembly of rock and cliff the heights
and feet that go round and round finding
in the smoke ahead the fallen trunk
the head of hair the lessening of its breath
a darkness comes the bell makes its telephone
a Delphic whisper a migration of syllables
nothing Apollo can *sing* will bring it back

(λ)

turrets of incense ! illegible cities !
out of the furnace swarm kings clans and scepters
brotherhoods of the Mysterious bearing wands
now green now gold and the 'sacred sheep in the cote
and furiously enlarged the Music Store loud
with its half-angels and abruptly slaughtered seraphim
chanting the histories of a single note throughout
the ages and bent over maps and fiddles
the midnight souls plotting and planning the life
this one the one we just abandoned and the doctors
looking through their myopia at the time pieces
predicting maybe five more years when in fact
forty eight hours and no more before the velvet
turned to rust and gravel and choking smokes
the leveled field where automobiles come to die
footnoted spirals to the legend of Earthly Hope
and in the basement below the rickety stairs
hidden bottles of malt liquor and pirated magazines
jewels and polished pearls scattered behind
the busted divan and a voice in search of vowels
and the incandescent ire of the House of Atreus
and the whole of Asia the fiefdom of some satrap
born three millennia ago in rocky Thessaly
where horses run wild like gods and storms
of raptors and divinities borrowed from Egypt
look to restore the pieces of their flesh in myth
such it is and always has been in the law courts
of the Upper Nile and prestidigitators wearing masks
imitate medical professionals playing trumpet voluntaries

will you please sign here on the dotted amphibian
and release your soul to the insurance broker
on the left whose subtle hair-piece and opium
identify him as one of the celestials come down
last night to drive your car away before the Flood
and I am Orestes ! it says a banner flung into the air
nights come and go and the maps crumple up
palm leaves wither enormous staggered animals
with antlers that bear the southern winds
no home is safe no life can flee on feet too fast
goddesses own the shelf-life of the stone and ants
wearing human faces drill through crystal in the storm
I say all this so you will understand there is no difference
between the language spoken by the beast and reason
as clarified by seers who live on air a thought
dissolves the brain goes mad the mind has
no corners left to round and it comes to this
a shoreline a dividend in shares a cliff too high
mewing gulls that spin overhead warring for a piece
of Osiris found in the garbage heap of Wall Street
our lives like scales misinterpreted weight and gravity
on either side and the hallucinations we hold dear
my love ! a class of consonants in clusters
phonetic decay and human consciousness left to bear
among rare blades of grass and shale
awash in the Delta's seventh mouth
turrets of incense ! illegible cities !

(μ)

we have been deceived as to our mortality
abyss of wasted masks and all the muck and lies
threnodies of broken strings catgut and slime
around our feet and no longer walk the mysteries
and sight comets with flashing tails of bright above
seasons come and go and names fall off the statues
they once wore like the one who drove his car
all the way to Buenos Aires to seek the oracle
blind as to aleph deaf as to gimel fingertips
that do the talking in errant dreams the mountain has
below we are as midges termites small things
whose wings have been torn off left to scour walls
and tunnels where they teach philosophy of the brick
a lesson in silent adze and dome the story of old Milan
where up we climbed the ladder of smoke and
down descended carrying unlit torches
and books we meant to read before we died
this is *once* someone said in sounding metal
and braziers of tumult in the wavering graph
red lines and blue that signify the time of breath
and the Library where we dialogued with stone lions
brought out of stormy seas to sign letters of despair
and weep into the cornice of this life a granite lobe
a shingle ripped from the palace roof
and figure eights that looped through Latin verbs
hollow the nocturnal sounds words stolen from a hive
bees of archaic melody that wound the eye
and nymphs risen from the marsh behind
who offer death in a thousand imitations
love and coruscating ire and the treachery of Zeus

smuggling girls from neon motels and delved
deep within the human fin in search of the bone
that Delphic dialect and flights into the preterit air
not far from Crete near Ida's nest the origin
of all the myth we need for tomorrow's on our back
the restless progress of the alphabet and motors
that run alone abandoning the burning wheel
a future without children and tombstones of air
x-rays that lead nowhere and the flayed moss
that lingers on the bark a license to read by dark
how great this sadness this welling from the heart
dense pools where whole cities drown and fireflies
abounding on the Platonic porch to write
the instantaneous photoglyph measure of the mind
that disappears without a trace in ethers
left over from the previous universe
flowers few blooming hues the tender memory
were we once here to hold a hand and weep
now restless hedges and fainting ivy the fade
of an orient made of deathless light
we go in blindness into the maze
you no longer *I* no more *we* who used to be

(v)

enigmatic poetry you say gusset and torment
dating back three and a half millennia before the phone
the quietly now gone and in the center brass cauldron
inscribed with owl cricket leopard and serpent
to Zeus divine this consider for all the oracle
and in clusters on either side of jars of perfumed oil
ideograms for sheep and wine and in syllabic script
the names for the goddess many times over *p-o-t-n-ja*
and the god of sea and horses the earth-shaker
the *wanax* gathering his clan by the shore in storms
petulant clouds gasses wild extra-planetary tempests
god-of-the-clear-skies in a wroth fulminating sun spots
solar thunder shattering ears of stone and marigold
and hibiscus and hyacinth in a circle to worship rock
fragments of vowel and circumflex accent sleeping
the depths where *Da-Mater's* daughter has fled the dark
crimson fruit fallen from her numbed right hand a
gesture that the world will soon end that the *Design*
is incomplete that what is heard echoing through crystal
down to the storeroom of the island is droning of the dead
nefarious consonants without cohesion violated airs
cannot be deciphered which side to attach the sibilant
imitation of the snake hissing underfoot and pale
gone the flush from her cheeks nor whether the …
and the absences and missing diacritics and difficult
passage to render and the light falling from cliffside
cut into uneven halves near the doe and roebuck who
scatter at the unpatterned sound of a goddess' foot
followed by the *whinggg* of the shaft sent flying through
the elaborated final asterisk dismembering the etymology

however false of the pre-historic numen who governs
flight and messages from the dead and all around
shadows descending twilight's enormous doves
mottled and indistinct tangled in ropes of wind indigo
as the persona of the *Soul* that sits on the throne
at the bottom of the alphabet any attempt to read it
fails backwards and arching up and the noise or
rumor in the mess bacchants maenads and satyrs
who eat human flesh and dream corporations of sand
that float through the elevators of sleep
and soon it is the radio and the phonics lesson in 1952
deciphering seals on broken clay (who was this *wanax?)*
vats of honey and dishes of white barley meal
the sitting around a brazier listening for horsemen
from the north or to speak the vehicles of language
like cars ornaments of uninhibited gods and *electricity*
lighting up the inner chambers the sunken baths
specters of woman transparent as silken sheets shifting
their *lamba* and *mu* across the painted floors
octopus and waves the size of distant hills and shipwrecks
beside the now long glazed syntax of men yearning
to sail beyond the western ridge

(ξ)

the heath purple bloom rushing under wind
to some still point in chaos the divinities of sea
and wave and above and below the prison-house
magnitude zero life expectancy null and void
a man's skin pushed to the limits of memory
distance and tonic accents and the mountain
on the other side of a secret script promising
salvation or numbness whichever comes first
the fair lamp it was hoisted on the ridge
and something else that cannot tell of what
went under the booming surf high as a church
threats and monitions and massive finger
of clouds and a childhood in suspense a thread
thin and red between glittering opposed stars
the fates or the furies whichever destroys first
each with their own vowel each already sundered
hemispheres apart yet so close at birth the eye
following what the ear hears the remote earth
and divided the floorboard between us until
I came of age to have my own stanza beneath
sloping roof and spread out chronologies of empire
in skeletal charts blade-thin owning to no future
listening only to the distant whine of motorized
vehicles speeding to the myth of dead cities
the necropolis with the most twins and a river
between its uneven halves and movie theaters
to possess nothing to fly as it were into skies
where the ether speaks Greek and strangers
don suits of armor only to rid themselves of

breath in jousts between cloud and airy fabric
would we ever know when the continents parted
the one talking hobson jobson the other pidgin
borrowed from the canvases of famous paintings
to abolish ! to eliminate the realm of color and
order and to annihilate ! geometries of passion
swept the galaxies with a golden whisk broom
told Mother it was all right if the stairs didn't work
insisted on heaving out the window the partial
index and contents of the sacred only Bible
wafers and wine periodic charts and drugs
weaving in and out of corollaries of truth
prophecies and pyramids and jungle languages
built on the speech of stone and rock and moon
rounding the heights with a bunch of rain
shapes and hands and thumbs and rigor mortis
finally the goddess of cremation her azure hair
her smoking nostrils and extremities of legend
skirts a swirl of flame volcanic ash zinc and mercury
and *children* too ! the fierce collision of alcohol
or the mysterious sore inside the hapless mouth
how many years does it to take to really die ?
remembrance is a paltry thing it lacks wings
it cannot swim no less run the extra furious mile
what can it say about the feelings inside the last
thought the membrane of sky peeled away to
explode with silver pollens and grains of
salty remorse of stars dislocated as asterisks
on the missing page and all eternity in an ear
zooming silently backwards into a flake of light
no history will ever record no words describe
the loss and shaking leaf of something gone
when least expected in the uncounted night

(o)

omicron the navigator's keel the slope and twist
of water what is rendered nil the fragments
great rock in sleep the various and numinous
speaking in zetas and omegas the voices far-flung
as sea-spume or lanterns just gone out high
on reaches we cannot ken the first and last now
ever and done foremost the ego's other half
in skies of secret plummeting over plinth
and cornice the shadowy veil harmonium of
nights on end in the second inch below the entry
to the other world a loft a den an inscription
in case of fire break glass and look at their pale
faces the fade and pallid look of all gone wrong
limits to the corridor and a finger here and there
tracing births of grass twilights in the manicomio
where orange and sultry evenings they lock up
and prescriptions voided by the x-ray and fictions
of disease and tolling bells I tell you I have not
been here before nor sundered the jimmied stone
my lives I have ceased to count and years like rain
go by in days and still the bed stands still and
monsters from the id out on patrol bear messages
if I could but read and ancient as the Hindu talk
about reincarnation is the strobe light shudders
in the bay where little boats of commerce rattle
gongs and fracture spectra of the ultimate beyond
so long says I the physician's fog and learning
curve the explication of some rare human kind
whose missteps no historian notes and walls erect
heights of living breath the pulmonary reaction

to a day lived too long to an hour over spent and
colors heaven's wild diphthong with a sorrowing
I cannot express so take this extra hand of mine
and shake out the dusty files and warnings of a siren
that splits midnight in halves irretrievable as ink
spreading its continent of archaic and hidden vowels
across the burdened silk of thoughts yet to manifest
but speak I with consonants in clusters of five
and twenty and labor to write this letter to alpha
and its little bidding the shale and shingle of a hive
where evening's intricate mausoleum discloses
a literature of sand and disappearing shores
the running text of epic tempests and sun-storms
homophones of cloud and spectacular moon-wastes
all the divergent weathers of a destroyed *Work*
palimpsest and palm-leaf shivered at the edge
rooted in a depth of tone and violated circumflex
whatever comes out of the mouth in trance tongued
vestibules of an oriental scale that ladder the mind's
small ports of call and dense and final spools
the unwinding of every memory in its shoes and
sadness of the door that opens up on eternity
when nothing exists but the last remote leaf
aphasia and silence of a lost universe

(π)

pneuma and shadow vortex and singularity
the leavening of pre-dawn light explosive
and silent as hush and shutters banging breezes
against an imagined window scarcely shaded
dreaming by the dormer's gilded knob a hasp
buckled in lesser halves the continent listing
in the wake of a mythographer's nightmare
one part nymph two parts hag on the crosswalk
chained to the bark of the three-headed dog loud
and swart its megaphonic howl almost syllabic
if listen closely if place the ear to dead soil if
sharing in the passage under and the currents
swift and negligent as to the ossuary they swipe
aghast the waters of stealing stone bridges and
cloud fabric of the deities who slumber on their
piece of Osiris all sand and tumult and the weary
head the heavy ho ho as if built of rock thoughtless
understood and fractioned into lamps of sound
shedding little luster of their history across the
aching chessboard and pavilion of space the station
holding forth in statue-speech marmoreal and lent
to incrustations of tiny gems pearls the size of ink
everything spreading a cause to the cloistered mind
a waking and a motion and the slow kinesis of a screen
folded over to show its own painted Chinese landscape
all bower and thistle and mile-high water fog pouring
its blowsy mists over a creamy patina four thousand
furlongs in imagination and the seers and mandarins
robed in jostling ire and pinks the splendid ornament

in the hand held high a gleam blinds the eye with nacre
fingertips of soot tracing a map of central Asia white
and failing on the embroidered hedge outside the
cinema projection of a vocabulary both secret and
oracular the divination of the entrance to heaven
labyrinth and pulse-beat of the human kind
unable to figure the way out and huge cliff works
and spotted birds of prey circling just inches above
and the sky rent in doubles and crashing diphthongs
that hit earth with a legendary and hieroglyphic noise
what ear what suture what constabulary of reason
can ever read into these puerile fantasies the loam
of forgotten civilizations flag and bracelet puce
and vermin alike swarming in a fan of bees AIYEE
the thrill is gone the identity of the singing pupa
this larval mess this concatenation of zeroes strung
out like lighted omicrons in the senseless prank of time
libraries and sidewalks shadings of persons on the fringe
elemental childhoods with kites and baseball bats
endocrine and subway trips to the place that never was
amniotic fluids viscera nerve-traps Greek synapses
wedged into the vague tufa of the Hesperides
what will this syntax ever mean but sorrowing and
grief spread out upon the hills of the western night
alas and gone the warmth that used to circulate
was called a life was kept alive and struggled
to survive but when it spent its finished breath
against an unreflecting glass it knew and took the dive
into the pool never more to mark the pellucid surface
returning its face of hyacinth and bright to the
nether and embrace of the dark *genetrix*

(ρ)

that was the night Krishna multiplied himself
for the swarm of naked *gopis* so each thought
she had him for herself in the round-dance
wet and dark as petals laying on smooth brows
is there any kind of poetry I have left out ?
out of which stone issues the vatic voice ?
discordant syllables about strife and order
and speaking in the cool soft accents of love
grass over earth and bare feet in assumption
to heavens of devotion and distance a leaf
or a single sound being pronounced in sleep
a different poetry going around darkly
between and through the enormous rock
jutting up from mid-stream around it whirls
of eddying rabid waters and the origins hidden
in each ripple and the projections of a face
the divine construct of Beauty the angle sun
hits first at the mountain top and vertigo
assembling the various poetries of the waist
or the bared white arms of a goddess fleeing
the wants of mankind and song and dialect
swirling in the bare dance of sufi and yogi
who will place hands on the Invisible one ?
tumult and aphasia of the oracular tones
dividing between the unseen world and the
unheard one the numinous and sundry gods
each an effort of the human will to *perceive*
and the tumbling forth of consonants in disarray
chaos of language betrayed by rhetors loud

in their information of symbols and meaning
syntax of the multiple mind and its houses
which is the poetry of the first order of time ?
whatever was promised by Krishna dissolves
in the thousand petitions to have back
the history of the flower and its yearning
set between thumb and index finger blooming
iridescent pollens consumed by raving black bees
and the airs suffused with mantras droning
the concupiscence of Œiva and Uma on high
and their furious and crazy avatars swart
and gleaming in the brain's jungle defiles
and the senseless chattering and dialogue
of mortals in their market place and harbor
plying the threads of discontinuity and epic
watching heave off great Roman ships loaded
with the silken stuff of religion and *Error*
how many other kinds of poetries be there ?
in the surfeit of love's altered commands
dew drops pearls of sweat and indignation heights
where the famous lovers of all antiquities *die*
to be reborn in the instantaneous flash following
thunder and the staggering rules of dissonance
gold molten jewelry in the eye and whirling
round and round the indivisible and *only* Krishna
madness to remember a life on earth
gleam of crystal a finger separating skies
to die after death ! alone the captive color
staining the indissoluble inks of the cosmos
an echo of light in passion's parted lips
each *gopi* a vowel in the rosary of silence

(σ)

you ask me where I get this stuff that pours out daily
infernally possessed by the Muse of disorientation
this year I have seen felt and known *death* to the very
marrow of what I love to the pith of the ornament
I call light *death* in its manger of birth the Lord baby
still as the sheet that lies over the sky just before dawn
it is outside of language remains without sense is high
and wild and maddened by a secret drug of *Sight*
making every day the Only day in the vial of time
death is the containment and the bursting out of
the hour the second hand riveted on the godhead
the vast and ominous ink that masquerades as life
in the midst of quarry and cliff and mountain peak
chalk and scribbling on the pavement outside the Bar
where the messenger of the Prophet gets stoned forgetting
what he had to say before paying the unrequited bill
death in its illegible integers and quotation marks
crumpled in the paper held in his stammering left hand
a situation like no other a slab of marble a beast
gnawing the heart within and the entrails and black bread
the glass of stale water the prisoner refuses in his dome
of irreverence and holy culpability waiting for his
portion of *death* for the dull knife that will not cut
and the warden's stentorian voice cites Cicero in
a great delay to rush the office of duties and delights
and the Greeks who invented the notion of *death*
on a quiet Ionian afternoon come to visit me at the door
knocking with their Socratic jaws and in unfixed
dialectic argue over expense and chattel and Marxism

while I in the skin of impoverishment can only nod
numbed with what I have seen this year on the last
day of the month of Fever and in the driving rain of
death and its illusive counterparts of unbidden sleep
and immortal trance lying there in a yellow perspiration
imbued with the balms of invisible and gorgeous crocus
the *Baby Lord Death* looking for all the world like a
lyric response to the loss of breath the imminent silence
that is the everlasting syllable of oracular stone lying
there in a meadow of water and longing and echo
persistence of the ineffable cricket in its bottle and
the hovering crests of unfinished angels promising
something in exchange for this inevitable moment
unmoored rafts and violated schooners in a rampant sea
waves of illusion and forgeries the heavens rent
in triplicate of punctuation and denial the thunders
porphyry and eglantine prizes of nomination and grief
I was given this for knowing *death* to the limits of sound
walking quarters of space blinded by my burning tears
section by section of air and the unillumined clouds
as I entered the five quarters of memory in the
middle a rapt and dissolved mind the brain of rhyme
ruined in its centrifugal volumes of pre-history
blossom and legend clinging to the remote hillside
where childhood first adventured from its shell of *death*
me you ask where and why the content is chaos
the mechanics of a single alpha in hallucination
of vertebrae in the darkened movie theater of oblivion
where each is the other always looking for the *hand*
to hold to squeeze to make palpable once again

(τ)

the letter tau suffering free-fall with world history
ca. 1500 BCE and the wheel synonymous with chariot
the dust-blinded riders and the javelins and inches
of newly founded metals and alloys the air a whiz
of cries and bloodied vowels and ointments and plasters
a modern memory cannot ken the elapsed shoreline
plenty with rugged cliff and isle kissing the flairs
and boudoirs of fake oriental princedoms citadel and
ballista and long evening tales about words encompassed
in lies about the deities on their midden heap somewhere
to the west of lyric poetry the blossoming of language
into half-cycles of sky and interrupted meter clouds
orange with the blaze of newly minted suns and tempests
wolves dressed like shepherds and prayers loud and
sigmatic in the orient of the women's-quarters a rave
send up by the altar waiting for human sacrifice namely
the girl in pig-tails whose voice emits operatic arias a wail
that will give the wind to slack sails and the remainder
of the story swords and epithet and burials by the dozens
on the coast and the distant syllabic entries known as philology
the crapulous fix of footnotes on serial pages indexed and
interred between stone lions where agape with oracular
news the Bard tries to sort out the testament of dreams
hieroglyphic and often enclosed in indirect speech an
emblem in crimson with hiatus and circumflex altered
so that it can be read by fingertip only while sleeping
the croziers and laments of the letter tau and whatever
else Hermes brings by way of introduction to the Underworld
++++++++++++++++++++++++++++++++(τ)+++++++++++++++++++++++++++

so this is an ending to certain and what stirs in the fuel and
sectioned off the wild air of Asia Minor waiting for Europa
the feast day of Saint Michael the village crutches the ears
of statues ripped off and the untimely gussets and ribbons
flailed and promised to the victor poor souls auctioned
off at the city limits and before the highway can be built
and the rhododendrons and mimosas thriving by the side
near there a water runs and hard by the clutches of nymphs
reciting cinquecento prose efforts and definitions that tally
a twilight silence the nostalgia and reverie of stone symbols
a tongue a thread that leads underground the bull-roarers
that bring on the intolerable midday heat and powders
violently red and aspersions that there is no tomorrow a
torment of verses and hands posing as orators and such
as it is the long hard climb up the stony path to Delphi
suspend belief! the beta and din of the throngs mingling
the merciless despite of the godhead a ruin of many cities
ant-hills dung heaps minions with atrocious names that
will never be pronounced correctly mantras curlicues
the panoply of punctuation and zodiac and almagest
the morris dance on the pavilion structured to hold
audiences of six thousand hapless citizens and slaves a
fist a cameo flung about the throbbing throat all white
and beautiful singing in the furious drizzle of light
by Hour's end and capacity for pity and handing alms
out to the stragglers the survivors of the great zeta rush
roadways erased evenings forced into taverns to drink
and doze and descend yes to descend into the dark millpond
gold flakes gleaming on the opaque surface nothing returns
can hear the murmuring slowly softly on the fade
pre-history of alphabet and death-wish

(v)

"is it tomorrow or just the end of time?"
Purple haze, Jimmi Hendrix
neurological rock fragments colossi hewn
from Parian marble and dragged across centuries
to the nerve endings of one's final years
the question is how to fill out the blanks
the space remaining to one's quarter time
on earth easing into the slots of mind small
thoughts intaglios legends miniature paintings
showing in bas-relief the byzantine ports of call
windswept sanctuaries where for decades was
kept alive the remnant and sorrowing in chapters
littered with the lopped heads of flowers
the once beautiful anthology hand plucked
with names like marigold or hyacinth vague
features of faces guessed at in a class reunion
half of them eaten by the moths and lichen
of routine and chronology the others in a daze
mistaking the clinic or rest home for myth
of a golden era eked out on hill-slopes bathed
by the tonic accent of a sun in decline
is it at once a sign a darkness of letters
difficult to read by the little lamp of consciousness
the sliding off the cliff of ironed sheets and bedding
Oh I remember you the historian and pettifogger
and you too with verses sewn into your sleeve
and the tattoo of faded and illusory glory
the day you ran the four minute mile
with a volume of Pindar in hand and perspiring

so many others mental projections
syllabaries and sybils and quarantined vowels
uttering oracular ruins of thought in dreams
did we ever really meet and encounter
the hegemony of truth in a few sheaves reeds
plucked from a Nile embankment and
Cleopatra at the black board and Caesarion
on his drug of rooftop ecstasies and once
or twice the toss of the I Ching a flute ceremony
or the time we opened the exhibition of artifacts
dust elisions and glyphs of secret languages
linear quotations of the price of wheat
in Crete or the dredged consonants of the Mayans
space travelers you averred and erroneous
but magnificent metals thin as wafers
or the plate-glass on the other side of the Hour
you ran right into it and through it
bleeding in a profuse elegy for dead poets
inch by inch the craven grasp of Chronos
cannibalism of the gods undone belt and girdle
soft instep of Artemis herself half-mad to
have at Actaeon and the whiff of immortality
in that wound and high above in concentric
flight the raptors waiting for the moment to
swoop and take their piece of Osiris
how you howled making up verse after verse
of all those who around you had already
gone like zen Buddhas in zeroes of alcohol
or peyote such a crush of figments
instantaneous universes by the dozen
colliding and collapsing in the hand-mill
that ground out soma and ambrosia
here , have some , Brother !

it comes down to this mere fraction
the imagination of light flooding the plain
dotted with traces of blind seers memorizing
the countless verses of the Vedas
unknown and not knowing and stepping
out of one identity into the next fictions
like you and I and the year-long dead
we bear in the hemisphere of memory
bud and leaf and dewfall on non-existent lawns
purple haze the end of time

(φ)

the nature of poetry in a shell washed up echoes
transformed by a hundred saints from the Deccan
eyeless and shouting vedic syllables into a stone ear
conjure that scene of a rustic night in a tossup vehicle
rotating its way into the jungle of stars appearing
without make-up on the left shore of the stygian dark
umber accolades ocher fustian warnings death defying
the child on the wharf who will pick it up and what
about the orphaned vowels the cluster of consonants
reddened and deaf from overuse the rust and cattle
and synchronicity of language and doubt the fusions
set off by cyclotrons half-buried in an inch of vatic
dust power of x and y to supersede the archaic alpha
switches turned on and off massive overhead bulbs
emitting a nature of poetry in light storms and arms
fallen asleep in sand and the image in levitation
of Aphrodite at birth fifty tons of solid granite wet
white-washed and reciting ominous portions of Epic
I love you, Tiny ! drizzle of sun over the Pyramids and
oracular devices set to implode in dreams of silk
and taffeta organdy wrapped around the poet's temples
boom boom boom ! it is the dawning of grief the first
ray of sorrow gleaming over the distance of *Distance*
to explore with a finger the intricate grasses of mind
the puerperal fever that ignites the hair of smoke
waving in the morning lamp suchness of the idiom
the brain employs to give instructions to the great Text
reading tender interpolations of mourning and setting
up on either lion outside the entrance to the Book a

single hieroglyph and the Flood rushing to assume much
of history in its labyrinthine water as is the nature of poetry
unwinding ribbons and soils and enigmatic Etruscan
omens and the signals flashing from each elevated Throne
and the several gods who united form the number One
ampersand and digit and pier a unique and distinct
formation which is sleep the size and index of ink
a variant universe just on the other side of gasoline
here and here where earth gives way to little holes
hives insect relics of thought vast and emptying verse
caught in *medias res* shipwreck and nausea framed
by stiletto and palm and the furious gestures of scorn
that litter the Tunisian shoreline three thousand years
ago and ago and ago forever adolescent green shoots
becoming in the Hour letters and transfigurations of
Memory and the silence of nymphs saddled into a skin
a song a threnody a ululation of many mouths in one
the months of reverie which are the nature of poetry
you know *them* who are the hospital and pharmacy
Cyclopean edifices of wind and sleet aberrations of air
solar syntax of aphasia riddling the ancient miasma
down here on planet X where divided by centuries
the brief and breathing semblances of *being* continue
making music and midnight errors and knees
which are offered to the Muse and in circles of heat
nine times greater than the summer that first bore
the nature of poetry into its river of oblivion
ever smaller and shaking the voice receding
back into its leaf and stone

(χ)

in the cave of sleep
the tipping spoon of trouble
the arc that holds the sky up
the recent harbor where Jesus dwells
microbes and fishes of transcendence
the global tapestry of the Invisible
what restless nerve and letter a story
tell the phrases of a missing moon
twice over the sheet of ice and beneath
a hell of fragrances and dynamite
each ink is half the quarter it used to be
a session with the Lord of Mice Apollo
and secret folds within the ear
where the mansions of ether dominate
and the myriad voices of grass
who speak and are spoken to by no one
I wonder that it takes this long to die
wandering in the cave of sleep
the dice and dominos that fingers play
the walls of transparent vowels that shake
an earth depicted on the other side
small jewels the gems of dissonance
a distance between thumb and time
smaller inches that insects think
and bring down a dome of bees
that swarm as One within the dark
bright black the furry buzz that puts to sleep
the aching soul in its relief
and beds and canopies of water

and sumptuous displays of memory
weaving in and out of rock
marble suspensions of disbelief
and sightings of Max in his ancient myth
the moment he came to be was
the moment he disappeared
do afternoons also pass unheard
disturbance of crystal in a microphone
long passages of space striated with
a crimson glow of Sicily and farther
out between golden flakes of cloud
and thunder that lacks a tongue
does anyone know how to extricate
the symbol that stands for immortality
an eye relapses into light and
light itself transfigures into molten silence
robes are worn for weight
and gravity disappears into its tomb
lifted high into the noosphere
a relic of the antiquities of air
can it really take so long to die
to transform a radio into a god
and take the dense matter of absence
and twine it fine around saliva
besieged by what haunts the mind
no sooner is it delivered from the womb
and thousands of brief spectacles
painting the walls of the cave of sleep
unseen the hands that wrap up night
unfelt the body that falls from time
into the origins of another
universe

(ψ)

the felt human dimension and its distances
where are the houses the bricks and mortar
the clay and wattle straw to sleep on and die
what is a palace and what is a poem
and when the narration is done and finished
of crystal are the heights
and of crystal are the foundations
but where is the transcendent man
and where is the puzzle and screw of divine nature
is it a music of Buxtehude or Charpentier
singing darkness in the pre-dawn felt all around
ripple of the vagrant and fleeing stars
if we could but see the *face* again in the morning
when the buzz and errant light of an instrument
that scours the basalt and ebony of history
starts its increment and inch by inch
a review of the past in stops and starts
a voice formed from a chiseled acanthus leaf
or a single letter carved out of mute marble
and meant to shout into the abyss of noon
a meridian of seas gold-flaked by mid afternoon
and the weary and lonesome and the gone
who have tied themselves to masts to *listen*
sweat their profusion of mortal error
each act is regarded with suspicion and hostility
and set the body westwards leaning against a wind
or the drizzle of sulfur and ire and bursts
of cloud ornament turning to dire porphyry
and the chronicles of mathematics and
the abrupt measure of ink on the dwindling page

I have been to the torment and back
and searched beneath the lids for an ounce of love
were it not for the silver price
and the agate the shape of an eye
how else to recognize the pattern and passage
the fulminating hour when trembling the mind
takes in what it can of memory
something driven through solid stone and
etched with lesser glyphs sculpted in sleep
a dormer of confused wedges and asterisks
incomplete the very whole of time
rounding out in cycles of heat and summers
of the daring finger cut out of grass
shaking in a mirage of hospitals and sirens
tattoo of echoes and the darkening coppice
by the edge of an ancient water and the image
of a saint hoisted on the pyre a blaze
of righteous ankles and pulse
who will defy the archaic heavens and
who will ask of the passing stranger if
there is enough spacing in his alphabet
for a tribute of mercy and relief
I am back from the dwelling place where
the caesars suffer in their niche of oblivion
sigma and tau of an oracle that I heard
the relining of the moon when it is least itself
and to wait for that midday of the horse
of the hands that shape and the mercury
rising in its swift course to *define*
whatever it is that we suffer most
daylight shorelines of epic longing an article
sent back after switching centuries
even if it is only a glove or a shoe

small memento of the earthly time
when it went running through rooms
not looking for but finding the relic
of its shadow the mime and outline
of the favorite toy the ringing
at last of the magic bell
that uncanny wake
of the soul

(ω)

"… forever that darling mischievous boy"
memory that loops through globe and sphere
to reunite with chaos the mistaken echoes
everything spelled backwards missiles and
shafts and darts three-pronged instruments
barking and chafing and ruined citadels high
above the incorrectly pronounced vowel con-
fusion between hill and diphthong the running
script from left to right and back again like
water lifted invisibly from its pool and the dark
underneath gold flake lace and opprobrium
and to recount in the great parentheses between
lives the names of the actors of the Mahabharata
each with his or her own heaven and ampersand
wild chariot rides empires of dust and infinity
each time a jackal howls and a new rebirth
commences in iterations of reds and yellows
forgeries of personae with complicated souls
three year old widows villains with gorgeous
manes like lions wounded but strutting over
a kingdom of cadavers followed by the number
two and its puzzling craters and hemispheres
circling the idiocy of economics and sociology
a knot a ball of string a labyrinth an adze or
an ax the skull in its perforated realities agape
was it born for this to move darkly across
the continuing x-ray of space and its satellites
a litany in phonetic decay sorrowing majesties
of leaf and hive withering in a decadent heat

if only as they all say *if only* and the sun wired
to its glorious steeds all swart and wet plunging
from the battery of light into the human maelstrom
petty unsorted chronologies of knee and shoulder
isolation of the biped from his yearning beta
to houses in disarray where night goes in and out
and clouds of engine oil and the bifurcations
of the mind just when it has learned to smoke
becoming a juvenile delinquent driving off the cliff
alcohol of Buddha-hood ! tryst of grammar and
unreason syntax of the modules of modernity
Satanism ! because the Machine has won this round
and the children left behind in their Prospect Park
flying kites and rushing over terraces loud with
color and celestial beams iris and marigold and
the children on their Flatbush Avenue and their
encyclopedias of Brooklyn and the suddenness of
whatever it is that stops and forgets to shift gears
and careens into the abyss of a Holiday party
faces and ice creams and hands all spinning out
of the control of gravity into a Hither India
where elephant tortoise and snake conspire to alter
the skin of fate the song the illusory registers of !
and the falling off the silence of a lunar eclipse
the oranges and shades of twilight on the last rail
whistles and yearnings that cannot be named
the lost and forever of

12-20-18

POSTFACE
"In nos aetas / ultima venit?
vitae est avidus quisquis non vult
mundo secum pereunte mori"
            Seneca, Thyestes

(a)

there is no such thing as history
only an undifferentiated past wearing a monocle
just as the styles of music change imperceptibly
so does man without realizing it fall into ruin
his health has visibly deteriorated he is no better
than a dog chasing its rabid tale the fix
in the arm this obsession for the salacious
this magazine of vices recounting in no order
the fates of Mohenjo Daro and Pisa in one breath
numerous Apollos erected on the stationary plain
looking westwards into the hills of yearning
and which is the one to consult and which
the one to avoid in the long passage
down the thread of one's limited breath ?
have I ever told you exactly how I feel this season
of colored lights and falsetto choruses praising
some deity who has come and gone unseen ?
with one hand I unfurl the sheets of sand
that cover the entirety of a Grecian archipelago
revealing nuances founts shades delicate limbs
porticos of battered marble a whim of thought
at least two or three decades of peninsular war
and a philological debate over the *end of happiness*
and on this the other hand in its upturned palm

read the hieroglyphs of a monumental scheme
the sky in all its austerity and chaos
and what's more the rushing between the ears
the interloping thunder and lightning bolts
that fracture the temples of being and the device
at one end of the tunnel that turns off the machines
and the switch on the wall that operates mythology
swarms of Minoan bees devouring the Mountain
I mean to be of them and following nothing
but the scent of honey and thyme and swilling
from an argent flask the booze of Bacchus fall
into the deep swoon of childhood the averred
nuisance and riot of the nerves no one else can hear
and I am of the world but not in it !
let us not speak then of the chronological lacks
in the Upanishads but rather of the texts written
in abrasive letters yet to be interpreted let alone
translated into the dusky hexameters of Homer listing
on walls of shadow and weaving between lives
the interlinear sovereignty of the Vowel
it is here beside the broken columns of Ashoka
or it is there in The Hesperides where articles
of faith and renunciation dominate the landscape
and the Spanish gold of so many irreverent sunsets
causes the soul to quail and I am among them
a littered fuse of characters scripted but
unlearned a hatch of divinities wearing sealskin
and talking bipartite riddles about the meaning
of death and the loss of the Beloved and the
ultimate and the many and the even fewer boats
we must embark and sail away with the songs
that have no present lack all past and surge
into the boundless surf no man comes back to tell

(b)

each person bears within the whole of the human debacle
each letter wears its own dawn and crepuscule
saying nothing but telling the same tale many times over
the marriage of hyacinth to daisy and the rains and
ruins of the oracle and the mysterious ending
in the crypt of fame of the smallest identity of Everyman
the laws of sandhi apply even to thoughts and nothing
escapes from the light without finally withering
a hand is dislocated as easily as the volume of dust
from its irreplaceable text in the library of childhood
and so it goes the et cetera of every day the nuance
of nightfall the endlessness of ink flooding sleep
the characters in their aggravated ascension over
the hills of dreams each the other interpolated
and divided and mistakenly reunited in a somber drama
wearing the masks of the forgotten figures of a mime
of overcast clouds speaking statues wasted shapes
walking and delivering mail and sending up shoots
to the erstwhile sky of Euripedes and all the Medeas and
Jasons on their paper seas raving up and down
on the boiling waters of ire and condescension
does the human form ever wear a different cast ?
where is the foot and which is the shoulder
and the ragged mantel flaked with weary gold tossed
over the back and combs and flutes and spite in array
what schollast invented Mind with its distemper of footnotes ?
down to the last minute the flogged disciple does not recant
and the story goes on to other legends and suites
motels on distant shores where mortals go to die

and gods too in their gusset and chafing silks all arguing
over the merits of naked Beauty and her surf-born
marvel of decaying radiance and the nymphs
in a glee all wet and sparkling doing the human dance
enticing this one and that out of shop windows
into the glare of so many hypothetical noons
this is it today the last of all eventualities and sorrow
each finger given its clump of grass each ear sewn
to an echo issuing from archaic rock each mouth
and tongue each pair of lips a vacant soliloquy of vowels
in search of their nuptial consonants but only the *alas*
of undue destinies and fortunes of the Mountain
on its other side laid to rest for travelers to recount
the adze and fork and tumbling spoon of antiquities
too oriental to properly translate and history itself
the single column of water spouting blindly in the night
daylight finds no drop remains but the faint of dew
the faded stone the serpent's shed skin a distance
which is the enigma of speech misgiven in its tomb
of leaf and marble the struggle of memory
to retain its shape in the midst of errant souls
too soon lost in the havoc of oblivion

(c)

photography of the soul flitting almost wild
to get out to begin anew to learn how to tie shoes again
to forge another world incapable of borrowed light
smattering of tongues hair-raising episode in ambulance
statecraft and plunging barometers did we ever ?
the thinkable the remotest exclusion from matter
what no x-ray can pierce the evolving sound of a mechanics
bringing the asterisms to our shores and setting up
statues of the divinity responsible for cognition
for the will to extend for the daily bric-a- brac
hardware of illusion come on over says I and
the ballistics targets and superannuated budget
allowing for a fraction less than last year's and fling
open wide the windows on Webster Street the fawning
airs of a false vernal equinox and mild arcadias
lawns and sheep meadows and the grazing pastures
of music in the fifth degree I tell you it won't come back
as expected only the forlorn yearning gazing forever
on hills the length of an afternoon hard by the old mill
the rock quarry and the deep pool darker than night's
oncoming summer storm the eventualities and
incisions precisely where the moon beam hit and
fossil injections fueled by hope the entire attire
hanging in the closet drawing moths not to be worn
again prinked out for a dominical season on the Islands
you and I sitting there on the fake beach of pink sands
waiting for word from the hospital about the effort
of celestial surgery to probe the inner depths that is

to say the soul's most profound and et cetera
the rest is like one interminable telegram received
about three in the morning you know the gas and
reflux and the can't take it no more of the human
lying there on a pallet by the idles of Athena and
some super entity descends with his glossy wings
and shouting real loud in late Etruscan *WAKE UP !*
but it doesn't work it's just all wax and a pox on the heart
and the walking dead in their suits of bright ether
talking their talk about the end of time the fuse
of delusion the drug and rifle club the clutches of madness
really it's just all about *that* you can't assume anything else
come on home it's late the Florentines have had their art
and the Pisans launched their last fleet and the sun's
about to go down hard on the coral reef whitening
with pollution and who knows what more can happen
dying is this elongated phrase littered with useless vowels
an appeal for one more consonant a note to sing
a frail isn't it sad the way it all goes out through
the camera lens the soul's utter shape an outline
a phase of echo captured by the click and stump
and silently passing out of sight an existence

(d)

opaque horizon sky blending with sea
clouds the hue of thunder pearl waxing
and waning without luster long sense of ennui
distant rumbling of underground current a
message some words from the effigy holding
forth at the end of the hallway a hand
almost rippling out from the wrist a pallor
that spreads over the once distinct features
the poem in its faint yellows and margins
fading from ink a whole world of lost
anticipation mountains unfurling like scrolls
of mists and waters in a landscape painting
hazy and vague the various punctuations
that represent something of the body of
the descent into places that cannot be named
the beneath of surfaces chthonic destinies
calling out from caverns voices of dead leaves
who had memories once who recalled living
a greenery and saplings on the ripe hillside
bee swarms and amaryllis blooming in
the corner of the eye which and what and
the variety of sunlight ! now turgid looming
miles of dusky and the fruitless branches
mangled by winds in search of a chronology
aching skeletons of air staining the remains
where cities might have been ports and derricks
lighthouses and enormous globes illuminating
a palace of two thousand rooms and dust
in catalogued sizes errant ghosts in fabrics

of fade density almagest of nail parings or
a needle in midpoint of an endless thread
whatever had been before in urns and shelves
wheat in numbers oils piled up for wholesale
dominoes and fingers and dice rolling over
the stretch of bone in sleep the dreaming it
was infinite when days had now lost count
what of the eerie siren announcing the dot
that periodizes human breath the woof
and intangible pattern of skies above and below
not symbols but the things in themselves wasted
in a graph of grasses and loam texts and
heights rolling over a sheet and its silence
prefigured notations of music that cannot be
heard nor ear of stone nor lapse of sight
edges frayed of syllables and mantras murmurs
inside the tumulus and spectra flying all about
in great disorder legends and flint of the origins
now collapsed in the struggling lung of light
far off and always longing the sigh and parapet
matter almost tangible fluted columns rising
out of atmospheres with the names of emperors
deified and turned to rust immolated and become
footnotes in the unintelligible history of rock
so many and then lessened by the minute
the twenty and thirty universes of *Thought*
all paling in the vast other side of time's
opaque horizon

(e)

and so it winds down fuzz-blinking death watch
the nine hundred or so and the tempestuous peace
that regards the passing stranger the automaton
or is it the concert pianist with the wrong last name
lost in the tangled wires of his own silence at the end
of the corridor where a structure wavers in its blueprint
I am of the anti-poets of the alphabets that have no
beginning of the those who have witnessed unwillingly
the birth of death on the third floor of emptiness
where neither the numbers eight or nine matter
a sun reduces its own disc to a hoof-print and noon
emerged from the stone placed in the midst of memory
hovers circulating its own history of heat and radiance
alive I used to be and manage the dark with hands
borrowed from a statue with erased nose talking
in whispers to the mistaken identity of its own sculptor
of them am I and loosen the fabric of what I wear and
lean over with some discomfort to correct my shoes
a woven situation in journalism a quiz in economics
a condescension to understand political debates the ego
of so many former selves the sleeper in a riot of aspirin
a logo a flashing signal in neon the brick in the mouth
of the guy dreaming at the horse races his bet will surge
and the so many gods placated in the unfinished prayer
a written request to freeze time and have back all the
losses and profits and skyscrapers etched in summers
when pools and groves and ashen moments distilled
through a panoply of lamplight I am there with
all those milling about in the thin wavering layer

the thirty third one of inferno speaking dialect
to the Etruscan tomb-builder the inscriptionist
the volume turned up to reach the stars where death
has yet to arrive in its newly minted ethers beautiful
as the child who whose abrupt month had twenty seven minutes
and can I look again at the rooms in a row darkening
gardens outside the fifth window from the left and
they talk of engaging satyrs and centaurs and other
fabulous beasts to do a recital at the memorial service
many pretending sorrow and grief and the hair combed
in a pattern of asterisks and the Boolean logic to determine
which way to turn when the road ends and the Mountain
with its furious innuendos of a past in sand and ink
look ! I am with all the forgotten the astray the set aside
the without margin the half-drunk & half moon-struck
the pidgin English and the idiomatic reduction of philosophy
a dozen and more dreams before waking and look again
I am the seventeenth in the last row to comprehend
that it is still raining and there is no reversing its gravity
holocaust of reason ! junk heap and nerve-endings a
toss-up of the hand a figment of a long poem about
exactly nothing figures of speech elements of doubt
the hero washed up on a shoreline long eliminated from
the map of consciousness that is me I am him grammar
no longer holds syntax belongs only to the letter Zed !
and so it goes death-watch pre-dawn sigmatic aorist
a zipper of vowels the lonely pronunciation in the dark
of them me going into the enigma full stop

(f)

the intermittent species called mankind
on the evening of the death of sleep and reason
flowers of an imagined hilltop the silences
and registers of a baroque violin doing its chaconne
horses of daring running the scales of ruin
interlopers in the shadows fusing gusset to chimeras
that evaporate stone emblems at the crossroads
where Hecate and her dog re-invent the dark
how much trouble to arrive at the next day
if there is one and the bifurcation of thought
because it cannot come to terms with the
multiple inaccuracies called history and
heat and the violation of the vowel in midair
who is doing the increment and who is falsifying
the message in the carillon five in the afternoon
ruddy the hasp and chain and the anvil
like a mirage on the celestial highway demonstrated
just once on the penultimate page the beautiful
copper-tone plate illustration showing the aegis
and buckler of the tutelary goddess in her phantom
city quantities of artillery and hosts milling about
waiting for the signal in bright red to sound
its furious echo and the forest of masts shuddering
in the harbor when will they set sail when
will the oracle be fulfilled with its simulacra
of archaic talking stone and visions ambulatory
of the manifold dead the witnesses to light
the unexpecting who were sent to the pharmacy
for a form of salvation and the hours spent before

the numinous month was up with its chattel and zero
the terrible and tender moment of *Revelation*
and a voice from *the* leaf calling out the approximation
to number the riddle of language the discovery
of Memory the myriad and disappearing stars
that dot the element of mercury as it rises
lifting sheets of flame into a winter of dissension
nothing can be reconciled all is left to the *Furies*
rushing about in their raveling windmills
accusation of ampersand and homicide condemning
the judge to nine hundred years hard labor
quarries and disciples of statuary longing and
sadness of distances beyond the reach of any clock
the tick and tock the minutes that no longer exist
a summer on the farm by the river-of-no-return
cousins and prodigies and smaller living creatures
lizards and darksome hordes of ants atavistic
nature of the bovine and sleek skins and pastures
the thing at the bottom of the well and its
postface syllable by syllable undressed of speech
ineffable meter and quantity of metaphor ascending
the why and the wherefore of the human spiral
elevators stilts and stairways capable of lifting the soul
but only half way to its promised land and its dialect
ideogram and homophone of enormous solar regions
where the *if* of what occurs after sleep and reason
are gone and man to man combat on petty fields
and the whole infernal disorder of living
telephone and wiretap and technological progress
in mounting plastic units that drown the seas
lonesome aphasia and dementia in the restaurant
the coming and going without meaning
the slender membrane of light and
finally *chaos*

(g)

who is it possibly talking through *my* mouthpiece
a voice a reaction in the mirror wet plenitude
of grace and denial the frequencies of error
and silence to wake to the fragility and the wound
no time can heal no hour understand no lasting
minute and flowers in the scattered memories
and full moons and tragic lessons and truncations
learning and unlearning forenoons among lists
of gods and ships and women mighty ballasts and
winds toppling cliff and house alike in the blast
of charged but empty words like drums and
tattoos beating rhythm against the silhouettes
hovering in midair like statues looking for a noon
to stand and plead the cause of immobility against
the darkened fiction of movement and tempest
why are there not enough threads to speak ?
make-piece versions of gloves and luminous
digits trying in vain to make a shape of the night
the ominous and the mountain itself in descent
from the highest and listening tight to the echoes
the virginal tinkling in its case of ghosts and gods
specters painted ocher rounding the bend beside
the endless oceans of time the great fluidities
in which we dissolve petty persons masks orange
intensities of twilight distances in an argument
over the next phase of space the yearning arms
unfolded in clouds or steams the fleeting vision
of an earth comprised of boxes and cachets
perfumed thimbles digits tumblers of lavender

wearing bright scarves of air about the throat
and to catch with the imploding ear just one vowel
one vacant syllable one ineffable homophone
sitting drugged inside the tombstone of language
and what am I but this plangent effort this one
staring back at the self who keeps early stage of mind
in a shoebox under the bed and wrings sheets out
with hands aching to recall what they meant to say
fingers infused with grief and a soil where foot
trips in the enormous shift of longing against
the tides and anchors of stygian waters a vacuum
where once the wain of love moved in the dense thrum
of life woven in and out of integers fading from
crepuscular afternoons shadowy versions
of characters in an unwritten drama about and
beyond the sense of *being* clayey nuances
that bring on sleep and talking and lifting weights
of history within the vault of thought incomplete
moving pictures overtures in cellophane crypts
with secrets of brotherhood and long avenues
reaching out of their asphalt into pyramids and
conjunctions of an epic style and final instances
of oblivion cameo projections of experience and
loss ultimately the yes OK that's it the finish line
and the golden apples tossed willy nilly sadness
dust and the equation of mortal passing asterisks
and dumbfounded lunar horizons whitening always
the and forever farewell the leaf in its memory
of shape and hue now indistinct formulae
written in *italics* on an unremembered wind
++
no legitimate use of reason can bring it back
the heavens open and close for the holidays

revealing gods too stoned to walk a parallel
shoe-horns claxons hunting knives and bows
shafts and hemlines and invisible ankles running
through forgeries of grass and underbrush
the comb and its intellect ! driven edges glinting
like steel in the enormous haze of fireflies
push it to the limit ! make it a line of poetry
a song of skin an indentation to park the car
waiting for the beloved and the rhythms of
hair and thumb always inches from the fuse
that ignites and smokes and divides the cosmos
into uneven halves of nine thousand dollars
each and the purse and plastic card the *Price*
none can ever pay and the urn and gloss
archaic perspectives of the deathless moment
when it flashes and goes out just like *that !*

(h)

from the ground up effigies in name only
monuments of air memories of marble
inequities between god and god and more
so between the living and the dead the summoned
and the abandoned those who weep not knowing
when or why and those who cannot have back
what they do not remember losing the all
encompassing reformations of time in a single
instant the thimble and the tumbler full
or empty the digressions taken with each step
there is no forward no backward only
the haunting specter of indecision and insomnia
aphasia that strikes the heart of the afternoon
lingering between the here and now and the never
all events are contemporary there is no history
drawing the fragile red thread through the eye
and doubling it back carelessly on holidays
who has been sacrificed without ceremony
and who sets sail on the morrow all a-tremble
with fear of the Unknown the blustery trade winds
the commerce with cannibals and devotees
of the Great Mother and rudiments of statecraft
and alphabetical lore and a smattering of vowels
learned by rote in a second grade classroom
and the slow and winding devolution of memory
each stone an impediment on the path each rock
with its peculiar incision each dirt mound each
ant-heap and the evenings that descend inevitably

with their grieving and darkness and the stars
fulminant markers in the graveyard of space
why do we go on rattling our scepters and bells
go on circling the self-same deviation of identity
and paradox painting on invisible canvases
recollections in abstract of a childhood in the tropics
one and one mounted on a scaffolding and three
enormous with its promise of boomerang and howl
why go on to four and five where is the psychology
in counting and what is the economics in stuttering
each hand with its own dialect an eye on the number
that revolves senselessly in the dry well of physics
differential equations torpedoes with the volume
turned way up and the god of radios and hemlines
manifesting a minute past noon to give orders
sufficiency before tact diplomacy before art
lessening of the tightrope preparing for freefall
the soul ! to understand its appearance and
disappearance its small verses in a whittled Latin
the subjectivity of a parameter in azure
techniques of the radical in math and sublime
the mountain of conscience reared up full
and wavering on the western side of the yard
where shadowy Platonists scurry red-eyed demons
setting up caves and ingress and out-take of wails
whatever could be defined by beauty as immortal
the shaking and quaking of the Nymph on the outskirts
of the wheel and the rubber tread and its hoop
like birds wingless torn from their hieroglyph
and sent spinning into the pharaonic sands
the amaze and the endless and the infernal alike
descriptors in the mirage of life the imprecise
day the hour that takes a month to put on its hat

the infix of the Sanskrit verb and the totem beast
at the end of the hallway lurking to surprise
the *other* in his renaissance of lamps
the time to stop a minute to die
the leaf the blade of grass
the seed of light
the dark

(iota)

on this knee the left is the domain
of human suffering and on the opposite
shoulder with its alphabetical metal
yearning for the godhead a spirituality
composed of high notes and hemispheres
so let us count small things between
the winter solstice and the new year's eve
grains to be numbered and soil in clots
fireflies in a jar that illumine the earth
at its darkest and the fingers on the
one side of the clock and the hands
that decide but cannot make up their mind
speaking for the those who have lost
memory of their brief careers in music
lottery of the stars gainsaid and futile
of vowel and consonant and elisions
and the pauses between hairline and
elbow the enormous spaces in between
full-stop and comma and the diagrams
and cheat-sheets played on the radio
days of rain without gravity and urns
and bells and small knives for whittling
heat and the radiation that revolves
in spires and chance and numerology
that governs which month it is and
which lunations to plant and bury
the shadow and its infinite hiatus aching
between hip and hip and the cuts

made for practice on the cranium
reckoning the distance between thumb
and its intense vowel of surprise and
inanition for how long that takes to
fill in the spaces above and below
the planet's wobbling course around the sun
focus and determination to apply
absolute amaze and skies thundering
in a cellophane of mountain and yearning
pockets of berlitz and verbal conjugations
irregular and useless as the silences
rising from the debris of Herculaneum
sad instances of life in an ambulance
so many times going back and forth
fusion of zero to the higher numbers
hieroglyph of depot and marshland
a stone fallen from heaven or a ruin
abandoned by the god of sidewalks
seas of aphasia spitting into the ear
why wake at all ? incisions in rock
and what is just as soon forgotten
rippling in a wasted twilight of rivers
that have run their song into the ground
next to the grove where Persephone
was last seen bare-kneed slim ankles
skimming the bottomless dark

the nightly escapade the fitter's dream
of life joints to be welded steam capped
insertions of noun and adjective side
by side the unintended vowel the syntagma
and eloquence of an hour in the dallying
spheres above where they make musical
notations abridgments of breath a turn
of the screw the leaf of time all green to
be spent in the month of withering when
they gather in sheaves of boundless light
the remains and swelter of a man's labor
the gnarled cork its branches aching
to touch the passing azure the undimmed
below they turn the sirens on and record
the numbers that amount to Sicily in heat
barking of the insane in their refuges
of wattle and clay the portents of myth
in forms glossed by scholiasts and pundits
in unillumined footnotes the intransigence
of the page as it appears once and only
to be read and poured over and forever
misunderstood when a man's brief ceremony
his equipment of alloy and subterfuge his
distance comes to naught picking among
the ruins of statuary and fane in the bright
when the hill begins to lose its temperature
and the shady coppice faints in drone
drum roll and Sanskrit infix the loud one
recited in the math of a closed passage

the Bo tree and its inhabitant and what
is found reclining on its adverb situated
like a god weaving grasses of thought
wind and potion and tossed seas in a bowl
handed out as alms to pilgrims of stone
the blind seeking the blind to necessitate
of the atmospheres a dialect of tempests
the whirling howl the indecent consonant
on the verge of entelechy and the immense
coda of space just before it goes out
the vast that lacks definition and coil
edges without plumbing like ciphers of
photography and tender illusions love
drugs antipathies of passion the nerve-
endings occlusion of the eye within seasons
of volcanic activity & lunar digressions
the heights where people talking continue
assumptions of living and rumored deaths
a why that cannot be answered the forged
intaglio around the ear the smallest mind
in its pattern of heat and rust unwinding
how red the fantastic pearl within its soil
the abandoned mine the shutter that won't
click the doorway in and out of the rope
wrapped tightly around the recent corpse
to keep shut the lips that want to kiss
once more just once the fabled moth
fluttering around the flyboy's frame

(k)

can the soul be dissected ?
a table to the east set with small gemstones
and to the west behind glittering damask
courtiers and ministers avoid the use of language
the immense realms of the mystic Union
open up with small febrile holes to the north
and on the south looking out on a great
yellow frontier like a banner waving
in storm winds a-swirl with dry leaves and bamboo
or when one reconsiders the dimensions of ink
the extents of dust in any given direction
or that the moon is a drug taken to eliminate sleep
and that for decades a single rock bathed
in a primordial water at the bottom of a dream
about the transformations of matter
or the history of space before time
or the inordinate and unnumbered planets
in a dizzy cycle of lives churning in a maelstrom
of illusions and prescriptions for headache
and whenever the mind reiterates its need
for a perfect summer afternoon and alive
the grasses and trees and the bending soliloquy
of the waterfall in a landscape painting
the famous colored quoits of thought
emerging from a stone edifice of light
elusive incorporeal and suburban the soul
using the dark vowels of the shaman
who has spent eons memorizing the *Rg Veda*
and can he say anything about analyzing
the soul breaking down its chemistry

fluting its indirect quotations clipping its wings
flight and fugue denied ! in a trance
music of a single endless note too high to be heard
the soul's Song ! skin and invisible tissue and
organs donated by the last fatal accident
and skies mutual yet exclusive of their hemispheres
to die and to keep on dying is the goal
the inexplicable chairs set up for a purpose
around the table where unlicensed doctors
gather to ruminate and muse with the *third* eye
of gnosis whether it is or is not a passion
representative of a breathing in the interstices
a section of the eternal ungovernable unit
or the unit itself the enigma at the end of the day
of one impoverished by illness who has lost consciousness
the soul is it nothing more than *Memory ?*
walk out on the boulevard of traffic
steaming vehicles of the gods flashing their metals
in the crude noontime lamps and listen
between siren calls and plaintive whistles
a sobbing a remnant of the echo of silence
the soul released from the hemline
unburdened by notions of property
neither the shining in the midst of light
nor the hand evoking its own *last time*
it can't be written so you can't pronounce it
it has no pattern you can't unravel it
without definition and lacking sense
however much you try to feel it
it remains impalpable and *sad*
in the tumult of talk and reason
a swarm of *fireflies* ascending :
the soul crazy mindless and
          indivisible

(L)

the statue abandoned by its alphabet
whatever comes to consciousness whoever
we are and the clouds of flies and buttresses of wind
the heights always so distant and beauties of life
remembered in their instantaneous measures
down here it all comes to a few brief wakings
walking around the town walls learning to pray
then disregarding the supernal entities
setting up altars signals a syntax of adolescence
getting into cars and riding in violent circles
and the statue first of all the homophone of Beauty
given its own alphabet its unique language
though never able to speak or read only
to demonstrate the antiquity of time in its model
of molded perfections outlines of sleep
in stone and the sheer alabaster whiteness of yearning
for whom meadows were invented shepherds and satyrs
a literature of hives and sutures and vengeances
corollaries of birth intensities of breath skies
the multiple lunations of prediction and failure
everything on earth reduced to a few ant-heaps
to cities in name only built on aggravations of dust
the filing cabinets of arms and blustery weathers
when ships are sent careening to their abyss
and the fomented and beguiled goddesses
for them the myth of speaking in trance and shaping
out of lifeless elements multiple mortal semblances
and the possibility of literacy and pages devoted
to the rambling cloths that drape them

with hypnosis and illustration a legendary wharf
where the mind of man is posited for an illusory moment
and the camera eye takes in what it can of
that historical incident the statue and its writing system
hieroglyphs borrowed from the world of sand
the nature of things intuited as a race of atoms and
molecules up and down the vertebrae of thought
to have come full circle in the dark and
alone realize the brevity of it all the corner turned
when evening becomes the last of the hours
and genuflecting the potential silhouette of marble
gazes blindly into the starry map and
recalls however dimly the once surface of earth
the dotted syllabaries of time the epicenter
which was nowhere to be found and the zigzag
running of space through its own loops
of bewilderment and ending
the unanswered enigma

(m)

yeah this is the bleak the dead time
of the year any year the darkest the most
and there are things you can't get over
and it 's not the next stock market crash
or the ripping tsunamis in another part
of the so-called world no it's not the gun
parts well oiled being prepared for the
next massacre this is simply the deadest
when sun hides its august head and ice
freezes the circling stars above and sleep
is on a binge to take away forever the flowers
in the bower and the sweet smell of hyacinth
or some other poetic abstraction the bleakest
you can't get over certain disappearances of
matter once injected with breath of the
varieties of air and color and loud and girls
lipstick blossoms cosmetics powdering dusk
the dead time the deadest the very you can't
come to an understanding why the windows
are so night and the frost is everywhere
covering the soft like an evil metal or rust
ores of the mind turned to tin sobbing in
the coat sleeves of a murdered mayor somewhere
in the earth of civil wars rapine famine and
colloquial for disease the ire and burning tropes
melodies of sulfur and cancer and the unexpected
totally news that comes seeping through cracks
though slats though old checker-boards about

the approximation to the deepest the darkest
most abysmal time of the year one month
after another with sadness and longing entrenched
in the body politic and the strikers gunned down
by the mobsters of history and the tyrannies
lauded for their acts of justice and duplicity
yeah nothing like this the darkest most abject
and the newspapers full of it red banner headlines
about divorce and ritual homicide and grief as
always the sorrowing the mourners Greek
choruses draped in the colors of planet Pluto
demesnes of the kidnapped *Kore* and loss of
anything that was tender with ribbons and dulcet
tones only this relentless waiting for the heat
to come on busted radiator pipes or the child
held to the bosom turning cold in a matter of
seconds and they talk of returning to the moon
or of more expensive flights to Mars the moneyed
and useless profiteers of Wall Street and what
of the munitions race and the strident efforts
to plunder the oceans and burn the mountains
all in the remains of our lifetimes for sure
this is the darkest season the deadest week the
why go on with the litany of and the threnodies for
and the nuisance of waking to another depth
another death another reported dying of such
and so and the memorial services in hiatus
the mordant countdown of time to its resolute
and dishonest and unbrokered competition
for space the lack of gravity the fulminating
messages in the heavens about the yeah this
is getting close to the end the deadest isn't it ?

(n)

man the visionary beast of impaired cognition
swiftly running through the numbers of his alphabet
goon shows and flim-flam wreckage of Holy City
on top of its own mistaken history of dung and ire
shapeless effigies rising from broken pipes
torn map of hallucinatory salvations and guides
to the *Perplexed* in the moribund dialect of Aragon
the letter *nu* is faster than the rest and dust kicks
up its empire of oblivion while lesser spirits
shapes of tigers or stone-carved lions or bulls
the *world* before it was written and the script
before pronunciation was serialized and the host
of numerologies and mantras intended to give
loudness to the concrete nostalgias of stone
atavistic performances of mind giving birth
to illusion and thought and the maze of hues and
inks and planetary organizations in a silent grave
grasses and summer heat the famous disregard
of childhood for the passage of events in pools
shadows reflections cavernous longings and vowels
eliminating the need for tomorrow and the furious
redaction of solar nights sleeping on the timberline
the body come back to consciousness then lapsed
again from memory element of nerve and bone
elusive as hieroglyphs of water recovered from
their antiquity by magic of Sancta Doucelina
in her proverb of tresses and quoits shimmering
just inches above earth stammering arms and rings
of hair coiled around each letter *rho* her face a blaze

intuition and fabric of celestial noise and if we
poor souls could come back to such a moment light
and sound and the archive of space and its abyss
and to witness the profligate excess of her tongue
reeling off *vidas* and *sueños* in an ecstasy of sand
how to return to a world of distorted chronology
and faustian lexicon of progress and hypnosis
is it by rock formation and hearsay we live and die ?
mirror image of the inner ear in gestation
reflex and kinesis shifting an insect page across
the bay-leaf of the Sybil chewed in ecstasy
of drum roll and tantric exercises of the Brow
networks of a single afternoon inside a fire-fly
and sudden loss of recall floating off the porch
listening to the diminishing echoes of last July
like a radio going on and off without a melody
and that is the moment *when* and nothing more
can ever occur a spear a helmet penetrated a long
soundless story of war between red and black ants
and flight of midges and things whose wings have
been excised by a penultimate roman emperor
a tax on the end of time vague unwinding of
soporific incantations poetry of dots and squiggles
meaning nothing in its entirety rounded off
by demands of the hand to have its speech back
apotheosis of marble in a reliquary of glass
cloud and foaming surf the *Birth-of-Venus*
himself the boss of booming roars his apocalypse
bringing the Olympian house to a ruin of vanities
and weary of his year the sun his hoary head yearns
to drown and have back no more his bright
though the days' lengthening to come begins
and the chrysalis its shadow sheds

(omicron)

divine or not so divine you are the Buddha
aren't you at the door of fame and time
a slot unspoken for the flame of cold denial
a fiction the inflexion of your nominal
the substance inordinate of your pre-birth
the time you came around knocking snicked
your knickers off and bumbled a graveyard doze
ancient I am you was a distinction without a gem
pearl was in your ear and shining roses round
your nasal shafts a grace you was and were for me
a thing confounded in the bliss of intransigence
phone call a night-some worry a fringe of death
extra letters for words that don't exist a sound
echoed in the tribulation of a trumpet score
unheard 'til the afternoon's wore on a Tuesday
retrograde stepping as whispers do on potted soil
or Hail all high the mighty vowel you were a
ringing and tolling in the bell unseen a note
the written air amassed around your ear the hair
and curls of ringlets and wringing hands
they were to see you as I was wont to do a child
a brother to the grassy knoll a sprite a legend
a water stepping twice on its own stone when
did you ever was Buddha weren't you in the
pronominal sense a string of noises a mantra
resounding its mountains of disarray an arroyo
in fact beneath our feet a dead-man's gulch
a pistolero with a rosary the fumous faming ore
that shines despite mind's decay it's passion does us in

it's wants to have what is not ours it's the thing
out there beyond our reach the glabrous concupiscent
dream is of being without syllables a humming Om
a somnolence in the spite of Shiva's shaft
bluish skin the four-armed forewarned deity of the dance
entranced and either eye was on you the Buddhahood
an alcohol of adolescent driving cars and license
and laws and treaties broken twice for why
is you so naked hard at the lintel breathing fast
the counter's off its scale and gravity no longer holds
you for me and me forever more the lesser of our two
the beings who banged about in the tintype jazz
the persons without a belt to strain the ego of
encapsulated diamonds in the chain of stars
whether the twain was once the One and before
a zero in its zed encore so swirling fast in my lexicon
a purity of space a Buddha at the very door a sequence
of knuckles playing fortune's dice a dying you
or me was there a fraction less for more ?

(p)

dementia the frazzled rock formation silence
the unendurable wail at the end of the echo
twice forlorn the desperate year comes to a close
or does it given the artificiality of calendar-time
the loosely denominated asterisms that pass for days
on this unforgivable planet that has squandered
its biblical plenty in a matter of a few years madness
of technological advance the stumbling hands
that create forgeries of thought and idiom
in bogus language schools inscribing books on
gesso and platinum and tossing out the content
bilabial suppositions of theology on the run and
fiercely devoured vowels in dream-space punctuated
by bull-roarers and dance between tectonic shifts
and magma and miasma the tortured epithets
of the letter *pi* a bibliography in red and year-end
catastrophic shutdowns of reason and logic
suspension of the Holy Grail or the pathetic path
taken by Gilgamesh tawny lion's brain and silhouette
regarded in kinetic shop windows sale prices
on heroic deeds and finally it comes down to the chasm
mourning grief sorrowing shoulders knees at prayer
meditating the fabric of creation flame hued elemental
as sleep on this distance of lawns and summering
heat circling and gyrating in the hopeless venture
that tomorrow will be better a bitter anecdote
passed from elbow to thumb and the grappling
with consciousness by x-ray and wire-photo and
tumult in the very verses of the first of the many

and the last of the few who understand that somewhere
in between are the deaths the unrivalled moments
lucid with instamatic realization that space is light
and time is the dark wrapped around it and all
the doctors with their savage precision cannot erase
the cicatrix of birth and learning and history
are addenda to the floodgates opened at midnight
the ruin and shipwreck of mankind in a thumbnail
sketching dialect and phonology against a patina
however thin of memory and the wet and perfumed
tresses of the naiads and nymphs who come too late
to grieve the as always just gone one whom the serpent
nailed with its mythic hissing a longing to rave weeping
in the fever of a spent childhood pyres of absence
the imaginary voyage back and forth to the Mountain
enough of the geology of mind and the tolling weights
on either end of the mortal spectrum a gravity brought
down by its own conscience and looking about cannot
index the aftershocks and concussions of the *Random*
that strikes in the night with its cruel simplicity
enigma and misfortune and bewilderment as always
and no one to ever explain the mysteries and why

(q)

the greater cycle has come to a close a moment
in the immense spectrum of instants radiating
from the *Logos* a blazing futility of imagined time
erecting on indivisible lines the spit of bodies
simulacra statues struggling with the gainsay of speech
only to flail with the aphasia of knees and shoulders
gifted with the poetry of hoax and idiom a frisson
of the tongue unable to articulate this closure this
I am the poet who denies the self to his poetry
I am the poet who cannot offer anything but
an opposition to poetry and verse and rhyme schemes
rhotacism of linguistic enigmas beta particles
besieging tropes and metaphors and similes
I am the poet who has no door to unlock who
is never the mask of the dream who is the poet
that startled from the trance of mystical union
has lost all trace of the *other* and instead goes knocking
on rebuttals of stone and rock the porous matter
that is its own ruin no sooner does the first line
come to chase all the others in an obsessive fugue
to start all over from the second he begins to forget
the why and the whenever and who was he if not
the suggested persona in the mirror the reflexive
pronoun the I am the poet whose intent is to destroy
syntax the order of sounds in their relation to words
who objectifies the plural of water as feminine and
who eradicating as he goes shifts blame on error
canceling by surprise the initial letters of the alphabet
I am the poet who is the *fulano* who begets histories

and rewrites the *vidas* of the troubadours using ink
the size of the Red Sea and fixating on the sphinx
and the pyramids of Teotihuacan and Giza alerts
dancers to the tumultuous hieroglyphs of music
choosing as partners errata and footnotes of the Muses
I am the poet who doesn't matter who doesn't care
who intensifies the soundless echo of moonrise as
the afterthoughts of fireflies swarming the porches
of a makeshift adolescence poetry and lyrics night-swept
babble spoken in the twisted ear of yearning I am
the poet the one who lives on the margins the loner
the outsider the guy third from the left in the back row
talking to himself in the medieval dialects of sponge
and arrow the vinegar of the *Paraclete* the anomaly
that cannot distinguish who I am if not the poet
of enormous disregard of nonchalance of banal mysteries
of the every day when the hour is long gone and the rails
are no longer parallel and steam and volcanic ash
are the true attributes of the celestial wanderers
am the poet of flux and disturbance of abracadabra
and hobson jobson and pidgin and creole and of
distant Sri Lanka the azure simian of writing
on palm leaf and x-ray the excessive and useless and
misunderstood of the neo-Vedic chants poet of the
this and the that of backwards I am and obsess on
certain vowels and not others and choose in the middle
to embark on seas of wax and stop the ears with sirens
the greater cycle comes to an end here where my hand
is the one remaining to articulate the immense greeting
of silence to the denizens of the volcano what is
the poet that I am as you all know my silent cohorts
my ears without conscience all you out there in the ether
epos and collision course of days without number

as I do no longer recognize you so you must now
deny me and start off once again repetition and
cyclical nouns and winding and unwinding the thread
the *tabula rasa* of the so-called new year AOI

(rho)

πάντα ῥεῖ

the *bolsillo* where you keep your hands is about
to expand into the fireworks of the dead-end of time
illustrative matter on glossy pages that remain hidden
despite the tumult of *vidas* and *muertes* interchangeable
and incommunicable as all insights are and still you
tarry by the vestibule of inferno pausing to smoke
one last decibel of tobacco and flute your player
on high speed the *inchiostro* and bedevilment of
poetry when it is delivered at 60 MPH racing
to destroy itself in yet another explosion of silence
the *Erinyes* tailing Orestes round and round the apocrypha
lamentations and broken spokes of the Wheel and
the great cupola of the Death-Watch a sparkle of gems
embedded in the eye and whatever else you have to say
only the rest is a re-run of the *fuegos* that punctuated
the skies if you are only sleeping the entire collapse
of civilization western or otherwise great walls with
their Chinese murals depicting heavens of silk
you can be there in dreaming the right hand can
catch up with the left were there no aphasia no fugues
nor the impoverishment of speech of writing systems
of abacus and worry-beads rosaries of disorder
beautiful and yearning for the correct vowels in place
simulacra of classical worlds marble temple distances
of smoking Olympus argent rills shepherds of noble birth
the whole apparatus of epic verse grammars of wax
and scarab and derangement of gods plutonic and

undressed warbling lyres fires that do not consume
afternoons in an idyll from which there is no waking
how else to explain this day of all todays the deepest
the farthest from sense the finger-play of nostalgia
dark green summits of irregular verb formations
piedra santa ! constructions of years out of rock
crystal fractions of the weeks *sombras* illusions
months that have been taught to fly like planets
while down here on earth the you of the everyday
lesson stammers a recital for violin and thumb
arpeggios and attempted harmonies which are
the wedding of tears and isoglosses to the homophone
of the rutilating sun in its ominous summation of hours
and you and the mirror of you and the scenario
where you are painted a flower in excess a blooming too
vigorous for life to sustain a marvel of hues and
river-runs reflections in gold flake on the water's
surface dappling and iris and inversion of clouds
how swift as the dragon-fly of glittering lamps you
were you were and then buoyed by nothing in mid-air
you fell and fell again lost of the wheel's turning
shimmer of bright mirage of fading you were
you were

(sigma)

as the light goes forth from the seed
and the arbiters of Underworld assume their seats
indifference be the judge indifference the counting
and loss of the weeks indifference from on high
or within as is the mountain so is the rock
and the deer and the door through which
indifference alone must pass and the yawning meadow
the freight cars rusting incomplete in their tracks
hard by the myth of the well and its bottom
ransacked for a memory for a tool or a device
as oblivion is the foil and from the grass touched
by frost and the dew drop in the swarming light
so the anchor and oxided chance the spoils
laid out looking east on the Tibetan hotel
or squandered in a sigmatic aorist framed by
grammar and its spells of rule and disorder
to speak as a statue in public majesty or
simply to lay the hand down that can utter no more
the book of lyrics the pages ad infinitum with
as guide the indifference of old age and horizons
limited by what the eye can no longer grasp
as the seed goes forth from the sun and the voices
from the leaves torn in a whirl the sum of
all hives and the lack and the lisp of the tongue
in harbors of forgetting where room after room
and the pill dissolved in the mind's antechamber
the abscess and the needle which is fear of darkness
to come and to pervade and to seep through
circumvallation and orient of the city whence

derive the chronologies of aspirin and marigold
reunion of the vatic forces and ringing of brass
in the frozen moment when night incorporates
the universe of the Unseen and the person gives up
the skin and the binding and the vellum
that held the spine together in an exercise of lamps
whatever else there is to relate but indifference
to pass through the remains like a sieve
snowfalls and footprints and soils upturned
looking for the archaic and its clue of marble
and ossuary and the reverend so-and-so preaching
on a chair in the midst of the aquarium
so we shall go in the afternoon to hear
and to be besieged by questions no answers
the fundament of indifference and the petals
gold and shining scattering in the portion
of twilight when the city evacuates itself
and ladies with their forgeries of love held
like umbrellas overhead and the talking and
the vowels in between the interpretations of echo
will you also join the forces of indifference and let
rule the days a calendar of moths reiterating
yearning for flight for wings of fugue and loss
and have nothing left to say
as the seed itself spoils in the vacuum and
whosoever joins to error the expectation
of salvation and the elysian fields and sparks
the letterhead asleep with flame and riverbed
always the unknowing tree the satellite in air
and boundless the indifferent

(tau)

speaking either Portuguese or Italian embarking
on the great southern seas called Discovery-of-Death
the thrill the-once-over the rot of the morning brine
air of whiffing tropics scorn of mortal attitudes
borne on argent wave and eve of the senses tumbling
downwards knees out of joint ghost of the spear
cast in blind moiling over weave and interpretation
of thread through the eye the courser moving of
its own over letters yet to be created the fling and
dose of a drug spreading dissolving the membranes
the almost Herculean the motto and mumbling
of the dream-arc a density to defy and skies unborn
raging within a pellucid lampshade work and dun
the triplicate paper showing off what an alphabet
can do the counting and not remembering where
one left off in the arrears of ruin conjunct con-
sonants wafting echo din of the ear's first syllable
a meadow of green riot a lamb a doe a rock sudden
in its aspiration for myth dewfall and ancient hoar
legendary feet with ankles transparent as rain can
this ever be the solemnities of a pledge to undo
to rephrase to pile up and throw out rust the troth
of navigation the intelligence of the unfound a mind
is it the spill of thoughts that trammel or something
in the light unfiltered that escapes the round of motion
flint and shale and the embargo on coal to the east
where dotting the tetrascope of ideas the future of
an afterlife hints of a possibility of an alternate
space a territory of wigwam and cliff and shooting

dust in whorls of melancholy and in jeopardy
language and its poor substitutes aphasia and mood
each person down to the last detail given inflection
a code for moon or Selene and parapluie of murmurs
ineffable intangible as recall in the heat of a summer
when movies were invented and the kids running
amok with their bean and ivory shouting in *Greek!*
the tense system and biblical verbiage all about the
Beginning and the Lord of Hosts and Memnon sands
and fluidity of cataracts where they lay the body down
and anoint it with balsam and paralysis sending it
out to the perpetuity of darkness O Thoth et cetera
and back to rigidities of the present and bees of entelechy
engaged in the reconstruction of memory musing and
the like a tenderness in the air a longing for distance
to complete itself without horizons in the oils of
a rushing bath and Cleopatra with her elaborate hair
like a city built of ink ready to dissipate in the steams
a wheel comes and goes the rotation of experience
hands uttering their digital recourse and the law
of inversion and profligacy how ennui how ruinous
and nothing to stop the iterations of stone and leaf
fossil ejaculations of light at the origins falsifying
the Word and distortions of vowel and technology
the finally tired absences the unaccounted for the
missing in their decibels of setting sail and sirens
of wax and entomology alive in the seeming drizzle
of sun and metaphor O Great the pronominal One
waters and more waters of recurrence and despair
always the moment that cannot come back or go
forward the concrete and ebony of distilled breath
gone and gone again me you and the southern sea
of drowning the sleep of remembrances past
the last and lilting the only and forever

(ypsilon)

is the world everywhere as they say
or reduced to only one place what we see
the abandoned wheel-chair the rusting three wheel bike
the abscess of memory with its remote lunations
hidden between cloud and sphere the rains
yet to come the transparencies of ether
and the boundless ovation of space leaning
on its right side against a broken corinthian column
the world that goes to sleep in its feather-down
scribbling dream notes to a statue
half-composed who is there in the dim pale
to remind us how little remains how much goes
in a trice the tag-endings of words dissolving
what could never be expressed what wears down
like stone in its water of passage what has lost
all sound syllables of the echo of distance
what lies in ruins the world its heavy head
turned to rock formation dense oblivion
when language no longer works the left off
left over the sad inexpressible constructions the
lopped off breath and conjectures of a hidden music
vowel and rhyme and sutures of air in the moving
cicatrix of birth after life and
it's all failed the what was meant to say the what
of anything that remains undefined the letter
snapped in two the sudden sense that
getting up from the chair moving toward the door
the animal sighted fleeing up the pre-dawn hill
the excrescence of something mysterious

on or within the body if it is any more
someone's to claim the cumbersome weight
toiling against gravity and winds and lamps
erroneous the faltering hand to graze
the switch or move a handle if it is
anything at all in the growing dark in the
dense and the unimaginable shape
left behind by the previous night aching
unresponsive the ear and the fingertip
and the relentless wheeze
wounds which none can reach or touch
invisible parallel worlds where lives so much
as the wing of a bee in flight looking
for its swarm for its burning alphabet
seem to ponder coming into existence
like smoke suspended in an unresolved shape
only to dissipate in a strange sunlight
dust motes flickering in Brownian movement
the soul's yearning release
incomplete unformed not yet begun language
unwritten homophone and hieroglyph
the sight is gone the end is past near
the only sobbing that shudders in the ear's
catastrophic silence geography of missing
parts digits rounded out heights the new
air the new air the gone forever air
as from an absent source destroyed
++++++++++++++++++++++++++++++++++
sadness , the and only

(v)

" siccus aerumnas tuli"
Hercules Oetaeus, Seneca

dismemberment psychosis cannibalism
gifts of the white goddess and the maenads
in their hill of dissolution which of the thirteen
and echo of the wheels that grind under
fierce rotation bones and mortal sinew what goes
on in the mind and the appearances illusory
and yet ever present of her bare white shoulders
the thoughts that maim the conditions that transmogrify
working one's life away in a windowless office
dreaming of spare parts of the automotive functions
if it will ever be redeemed and the springtime
of the faun and the corollaries of greens the
intaglios and ribbing of the leaf-design pressed
against rock crystal and what passes for history
in the winding spools of Lachesis and formidable
what goes on in the mind and treads the water
of darkness and why were you up there
chasing that sylph when you should have been
paying your taxes like a decent citizen reading
instead the Italian masters the Troubadours
vidas and dalliance of overseas loves the imagined
happenings that riot the brain transept and fugue
and whatever else to ward off the aging process
dreaming syntax of the unimaginable up there
weaving wave over lawn and shadows of whatever
can be the system the mind sets up and you prowl

night streets alleyways dichotomies of soil
and stone the sandy reaches of some outer province
to govern with donkey and trellis and promise
to never touch her again and the forbidding
principles of law and order insanity of the linear
sleeping head deep in unreason and fiction
will it ever come to pass the Mountain and
its prolific byways of literature and semaphores
likewise you say answering an unseen tormentor
born of the mind and its unsettling vowels
colossal statues works of the untrammeled
or relearning the Greek and alphabetical revisions
madness and the psyche of cave and terror
one of the thirteen will be there a finger wet
with dross and ink a script unfurled in the sirocco
of her breath leading you on to the death
after death to the being without contours
to the really insane projections of what a mind
can illustrate in its panoply of derelict dreams
the dance and the toreador and the roaring from
the oven in its small hours of process burning
words and reflections and ultimately the endings
tragic and sorrow and grieving what you must
take with you and cannot distribute but
to your lonesome self the ruin *mind*

(w)

mythic the really grand and words proliferate
soundless into the smoking gestures a hand
reaching out of the clouds the serenity of Olympus
ivory tacked onto ebony rivers of the beneath
a world of symbols in the swirl of coming-to-be
each who is really the *other* reaching forwards
into the past with a sinew of illusions a syntax of
riddles constituting memory of the undergone
and seas right outside the window and apocalypse
waking from the edge and looking for a name
in the plethora of scripts half deciphered or
not at all but question marks illegible squiggles
the echo of Hammurabi in the middle decoded
furnished room on the Tigris circa 2500BCE
dumbfounded *sombras* fixtures in italics or
simply vowels discordant in isolation from
meaning mirrored backwards in Etruscan
glass and the tiny hegemony of the jeweled eye
in the court of Ferrara centuries in the future
slippered feet in soft felt and the cry for carrion
the ongoing wars for dominion of the clock
the edifice of fire and the Hour of reflection
whoever can wake from this and recount syllable
by syllable what the Sybil in her bottle said
descriptors and chanting the ear muzzled in
its insane meridian of apology and heat waves
for why am I so forlorn for why is this *me* ?
shelled and pistoned the aggravation of time
its minor occurrences of idiom and ego the

finally greater years with their unnamed planets
orbits of nonesuch whirring of millponds muss
and folly of the oracle emerging from unities
of stone and nightmare the vision foremost
of a teleology of walls and statues yearning
for hands to hold for voices to yield to winds
a book at a time fossil relics of salt and foam
around eddying births of gleaming divinities
indexed in the encyclopedia of wheel and return
OK so the mayhap and occasion don't match
with the summer's finalized month the obituary
of sand the false notice of ordeal by shoulder
progression of the inch of ink through dialect
swamp and turmoil inhalation of Pluto
why do they not take better photos to capture
the insect on the lam to break up the hiatus
formed by treaties with Athens and the democrats
and am I then on the thither side of time ?
an alarm of twins gongs and gas beakers
exploding minutely the floorboards and tins
of alchemy the far-reaching surrealism
by definition of the world's first fire engine
and we stand agog at the edge of a moving cliff
oceans of space far-flung entities dots and punts
realization of a kinetic screen a sorrowing and
disorder before its hour and why couldn't just
one more bracket have saved the child *why ?*

(x)

bow we then to the *Magna Mater* of Crete *her* is
residual of the light in faint gold flakes surfacing
and winter too is in stone and in the gravity of air
either arm is a serpent and the bright in the eyes
sapphire or the cold spray of dissolving pearl
that come dancing over painted pools of water
meant to resemble distance and the palaces where
winds are born to fly and flay in all directions
nor will the sailor survive his night nor plowman
his stubborn ox fell before daybreak and all is
a ruin a history of misinterpretations and bees
that swarm the gimlet and the rushing flank
somewhere in a parallel orient of broken dawns
lay we down the heavy head on this icy parapet
and let the goddess open the heart's casing *Lo !*
imps and scarabs and winged signs that pattern
sleep's enormous inky map and do walls fall
the names of cities die in the ear and cardboard
figurines cutting eights out of hewn marble
meant to repose as statuary at the gate and gongs
that mutilate hearing with lack of concord
harmony of vowels consonantal overtures to words
chiseled out of the sibyl's deranged tongue we do
performing rites of blood and áãáðç moving as
silk over damp summer skin an afternoon of fauns
of celestial bowers draped in a premature dark
stealth of language to deceive and benight in folios
and incunabula and phases of the moon in rapid
succession thumbed and printed on grass labels

to suffer what else occurs in this aorist tense a
false memory an evocation of the *chaste* One
who runs her slim feet in an epiphany over rock
aiming fate in the startled chase of her vestments
white on white and the lapse of red in vague
sentiments if to look at the nocturnal sky is to
absent the self of its parameters and syllabaries
we are come to naught and knees razed by flint
and shoulders in an attitude of perpetual grief
haunted by the hive where mind keeps its thoughts
of living that we can no longer enter the street
for the electric buzzing loud in the clarity
aware but not conscious of the happenings many
as are the variations of a single archaic fable of
meter and tone and linguistic inference of the psyche
and however multitudinous the stars may appear
they are but hallucinatory splotches dots faint
as the folk who dwell in cliffs or those who spark
riots in the intellect and foment ire cursing
birth and fortune and who ill are faint and
pale the longing and hazard of twilight fading
not reason but the sound that is never heard
                              Magna Mater's weeping
in a haste to bring confusion to the houses of
the heavens clouds veins and ribbings shot
in a cinema of the ancient and fossil air
the sorrows that define mortal lives

(y)

are there conjunct consonants on the sun ?
what is the syntax of the competing winds ?
what if the mind can ever come home again ?
lexica of the ineffable ! *fire sage poet enemy king*
and so it goes through the first and last stages
before sleep was invented and after sleep
was eliminated vowels of smoke strung out
like a dissolving rosary prayers of unspoken
alphanumerical sorrows on a shifting grid
interpolar asterisms and asterisks and doubts
can *one* and *one* ever add up ? think thoughts
that can never be uttered speak in tones of
absolute heights the edges of sanity the shelves
where brain sits waiting to expire or explode
which of the native brooks of reason is viable ?
questions leave their marks on the syllabary
that no hands can hold no page can turn no
nothing only the horizon of a legend of waters
rising by the inch into a neolithic deluge that
covers all the surfaces of all the words ever *ever !*
I am the concupiscence of the letter zed for once
and never more and tread the soft issues of beta
and trammel the exits of gamma and delta
and talk and only to the aphasics in the library
whose knees and pulses stammer code to
pharmacists disguised as metaphysicians
the loud unequivocal noon of their foreheads
ablaze with emerging pre-socratic cosmogonies
freighted with grief for all the years survived

do I now want to enter the lists of the many *who*
and leave it at that a probability of darkness
before the hour even begins a sliver of moon
a slab of marble in the alchemical kitchen
it's the end every time I open the rule-book
everywhere it says you have to do it this way
and no other and I am always on the other
side of righteousness and justice expecting
the funeral parlor to call back and say it was
all a big mistake you can have the body back
though some of the gussets and ribbons are missing
you can have the body back but not the soul
it escaped already too soon eager for light
and space-flight and the endlessness
of a long forgotten childhood

(z)

my father as always where it ends painting
every day of his life profligate sinner and mystic
caressing gravel and coloring the rocks around it
and sanctifying binges and acts of moral turpitude
by pushing the excesses of art to the walls of
both hotel-bar and nunnery and playing in solitude
the piano three in the morning with *San Juan de la Cruz*
a figure remote terrifying and to be admired living
out his musical Mexican losses in the far woods
of northern Minnehaha when all the while his heart
was in Guadalajara a riot of revolution and mariachi
as always ending where my father was and is a
painting of rocks and gravel and alcohol
in basements and taverns Sunday afternoons
alien from the south of the frontera *guapo* and far
from the mountain of reason his solitude in a piano
with *San Juan de la Cruz* three in the morning walls
and wails of and nunneries and bitter cold of newspaper
predictions and cold wars and fusion of booze and
calendar art brought to his knees mugging holy men
es mi culpa ! es mi culpa ! knowing when and if was
to die in far northern wood intricacies of word-play
doubting orthography and pronunciation and mockery
of all that is plebeian and the phrases of his brilliant
mind tattooed in the air with silver Aztec masks and
legends of Trotsky's brains forceful attitude and
melodies *Perfidia* knocking down illusory prejudices
with his Clark Gable smile the women adored him
rogue and impossible lover hidden in secret trenches

of glossy magazine pages and who wouldn't turn
him out after midnight or put him in the hoosegow
inveterate boozer with slicked down Latino hair
parted right where the Sierra Madre dips into the
sea a thousand miles from anyone's idea of love
in his arms dying mother and relics of Guadalupe
tainted carburetors mish-mash of automobile parts
guitar soliloquys and painted gardens of a paradise
that existed for a little over a year in Culver City
honking the horn for his Honey ever elusive paternity
shunned wishing it were all over back there in
some dingy bar in DF playing in a trio *Bésame mucho*
instead of shoveling snow mounds the size of
a third world banana republic in frozen wastes
where Hiawatha's tortured spirit ululates Mississippi
infernos backdrop of tiny German Lutheran hamlets
posters of coke drinking models peeling off fragmented
outhouses where nothing really matters an ending
to him to this to poetry to the land of sky blue *Waters*
postfaced endings to language to inhibitions of speech
to statues begging for tongues and sight for writing
the over and over again
and out
zero
ándale pues !

01-06-19
Berkeley CA